D0462775

Field Guide to Hadoop

Kevin Sitto and Marshall Presser

Beijing · Cambridge · Farnham · Köln · Sebastopol · Tokyo

Field Guide to Hadoop

by Kevin Sitto and Marshall Presser

Published by O'Reilly Media, Inc., 1005 Gravenstein Highway North, Sebastopol, CA 95472.

O'Reilly books may be purchased for educational, business, or sales promotional use. Online editions are also available for most titles (*http://safaribooksonline.com*). For more information, contact our corporate/institutional sales department: 800-998-9938 or *corporate@oreilly.com*.

Editors: Mike Loukides and Shannon Cutt	**Proofreader:** Amanda Kersey
Production Editor: Kristen Brown	**Interior Designer:** David Futato
Copyeditor: Jasmine Kwityn	**Cover Designer:** Ellie Volckhausen
	Illustrator: Rebecca Demarest

March 2015:   First Edition

Revision History for the First Edition
2015-02-27:   First Release

See *http://oreilly.com/catalog/errata.csp?isbn=9781491947937* for release details.

978-1-491-94793-7

[LSI]

To my beautiful wife, Erin, for her endless patience, and my wonderful children, Dominic and Ivy, for keeping me in line.

—Kevin

To my wife, Nancy Sherman, for all her encouragement during our writing, rewriting, and then rewriting yet again. Also, many thanks go to that cute little yellow elephant, without whom we wouldn't even have thought about writing this book.

—Marshall

Table of Contents

Preface

What is Hadoop and why should you care? This book will help you understand what Hadoop is, but for now, let's tackle the second part of that question. Hadoop is the most common single platform for storing and analyzing big data. If you and your organization are entering the exciting world of big data, you'll have to decide whether Hadoop is the right platform and which of the many components are best suited to the task. The goal of this book is to introduce you to the topic and get you started on your journey.

There are many books, websites, and classes about Hadoop and related technologies. This one is different. It does not provide a lengthy tutorial introduction to a particular aspect of Hadoop or to any of the many components of the Hadoop ecosystem. It certainly is not a rich, detailed discussion of any of these topics. Instead, it is organized like a field guide to birds or trees. Each chapter focuses on portions of the Hadoop ecosystem that have a common theme. Within each chapter, the relevant technologies and topics are briefly introduced: we explain their relation to Hadoop and discuss why they may be useful (and in some cases less than useful) for particular needs. To that end, this book includes various short sections on the many projects and subprojects of Apache Hadoop and some related technologies, with pointers to tutorials and links to related technologies and processes.

In each section, we have included a table that looks like this:

License	<License here>
Activity	None, Low, Medium, High
Purpose	<Purpose here>
Official Page	<URL>
Hadoop Integration	Fully Integrated, API Compatible, No Integration, Not Applicable

Let's take a deeper look at what each of these categories entails:

License

While all of the sections in the first version of this field guide are open source, there are several different licenses that come with the software—mostly alike, with some differences. If you plan to include this software in a product, you should familiarize yourself with the conditions of the license.

Activity

We have done our best to measure how much active development work is being done on the technology. We may have misjudged in some cases, and the activity level may have changed since we first wrote on the topic.

Purpose

What does the technology do? We have tried to group topics with a common purpose together, and sometimes we found that a topic could fit into different chapters. Life is about making choices; these are the choices we made.

Official Page

If those responsible for the technology have a site on the Internet, this is the home page of the project.

Hadoop Integration

When we started writing, we weren't sure exactly what topics we would include in the first version. Some on the initial list were tightly integrated or bound into Apache Hadoop. Others were alternative technologies or technologies that worked with Hadoop but were not part of the Apache Hadoop family. In those cases, we tried to best understand what the level of integration was at the time of our writing. This will no doubt change over time.

You should not think that this book is something you read from cover to cover. If you're completely new to Hadoop, you should start by reading the introductory chapter, Chapter 1. Then you should look for topics of interest, read the section on that component, read the chapter header, and possibly scan other selections in the same chapter. This should help you get a feel for the subject. We have often included links to other sections in the book that may be relevant. You may also want to look at links to tutorials on the subject or to the "official" page for the topic.

We've arranged the topics into sections that follow the pattern in the diagram shown in Figure P-1. Many of the topics fit into the Hadoop Common (formerly the Hadoop Core), the basic tools and techniques that support all the other Apache Hadoop modules. However, the set of tools that play an important role in the big data ecosystem isn't limited to technologies in the Hadoop core. In this book we also discuss a number of related technologies that play a critical role in the big data landscape.

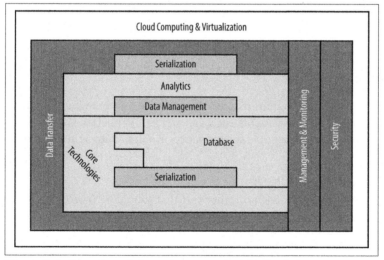

Figure P-1. Overview of the topics covered in this book

In this first edition, we have not included information on any proprietary Hadoop distributions. We realize that these projects are important and relevant, but the commercial landscape is shifting so quickly that we propose a focus on open source technology only.

Open source has a strong hold on the Hadoop and big data markets at the moment, and many commercial solutions are heavily based on the open source technology we describe in this book. Readers who are interested in adopting the open source technologies we discuss are encouraged to look for commercial distributions of those technologies if they are so inclined.

This work is not meant to be a static document that is only updated every year or two. Our goal is to keep it as up to date as possible, adding new content as the Hadoop environment grows and some of the older technologies either disappear or go into maintenance mode as they become supplanted by others that meet newer technology needs or gain in favor for other reasons.

Since this subject matter changes very rapidly, readers are invited to submit suggestions and comments to Kevin (*ksitto@gmail.com*) and Marshall (*bigmaish@gmail.com*). Thank you for any suggestions you wish to make.

Conventions Used in This Book

The following typographical conventions are used in this book:

Italic
> Indicates new terms, URLs, email addresses, filenames, and file extensions.

`Constant width`
> Used for program listings, as well as within paragraphs to refer to program elements such as variable or function names, databases, data types, environment variables, statements, and keywords.

`Constant width bold`
> Shows commands or other text that should be typed literally by the user.

`Constant width italic`
> Shows text that should be replaced with user-supplied values or by values determined by context.

Safari® Books Online

Safari Books Online is an on-demand digital library that delivers expert content in both book and video form from the world's leading authors in technology and business.

Technology professionals, software developers, web designers, and business and creative professionals use Safari Books Online as their primary resource for research, problem solving, learning, and certification training.

Safari Books Online offers a range of plans and pricing for enterprise, government, education, and individuals.

Members have access to thousands of books, training videos, and prepublication manuscripts in one fully searchable database from publishers like O'Reilly Media, Prentice Hall Professional, Addison-Wesley Professional, Microsoft Press, Sams, Que, Peachpit Press, Focal Press, Cisco Press, John Wiley & Sons, Syngress, Morgan Kaufmann, IBM Redbooks, Packt, Adobe Press, FT Press, Apress, Manning, New Riders, McGraw-Hill, Jones & Bartlett, Course Technology, and hundreds more. For more information about Safari Books Online, please visit us online.

How to Contact Us

Please address comments and questions concerning this book to the publisher:

> O'Reilly Media, Inc.
> 1005 Gravenstein Highway North
> Sebastopol, CA 95472
> 800-998-9938 (in the United States or Canada)
> 707-829-0515 (international or local)
> 707-829-0104 (fax)

We have a web page for this book, where we list errata, examples, and any additional information. You can access this page at *http://bit.ly/field-guide-hadoop*.

To comment or ask technical questions about this book, send email to *bookquestions@oreilly.com*.

For more information about our books, courses, conferences, and news, see our website at *http://www.oreilly.com*.

Find us on Facebook: *http://facebook.com/oreilly*

Follow us on Twitter: *http://twitter.com/oreillymedia*

Watch us on YouTube: *http://www.youtube.com/oreillymedia*

Acknowledgments

We'd like to thank our reviewers Harry Dolan, Michael Park, Don Miner, and Q Ethan McCallum. Your time, insight, and patience are incredibly appreciated.

We also owe a big debt of gratitude to the team at O'Reilly for all their help. We'd especially like to thank Mike Loukides for his invaluable help as we were getting started, Ann Spencer for helping us think more clearly about how to write a book, and Shannon Cutt, whose comments made this work possible. A special acknowledgment to Rebecca Demarest and Dan Fauxsmith for all their help.

We'd also like to give a special thanks to Paul Green for teaching us about big data before it was "a thing" and to Don Brancato for forcing a coder to read Strunk & White.

CHAPTER 1
Core Technologies

In 2002, when the World Wide Web was relatively new and before you "Googled" things, Doug Cutting and Mike Cafarella wanted to crawl the Web and index the content so that they could produce an Internet search engine. They began a project called Nutch to do this but needed a scalable method to store the content of their indexing. The standard method to organize and store data in 2002 was by means of relational database management systems (RDBMS), which were accessed in a language called SQL. But almost all SQL and relational stores were not appropriate for Internet search engine storage and retrieval. They were costly, not terribly scalable, not as tolerant to failure as required, and possibly not as performant as desired.

In 2003 and 2004, Google released two important papers, one on the Google File System (*http://bit.ly/1CgWGTy*)[1] and the other on a programming model on clustered servers called MapReduce (*http://bit.ly/12c3Ifq*).[2] Cutting and Cafarella incorporated these technologies into their project, and eventually Hadoop was born. Hadoop is not an acronym. Cutting's son had a yellow stuffed elephant he named Hadoop, and somehow that name stuck to the project and the icon is a cute little elephant. Yahoo! began using Hadoop as the

---

1 Sanjay Ghemawat, Howard Gobioff, and Shun-Tak Leung, "The Google File System," *Proceedings of the Nineteenth ACM Symposium on Operating Systems Principles - SOSP '03* (2003): 29-43.

2 Jeffrey Dean and Sanjay Ghemawat, "MapReduce: Simplified Data Processing on Large Clusters," *Proceedings of the 6th Conference on Symposium on Operating Systems Design and Implementation* (2004).

basis of its search engine, and soon its use spread to many other organizations. Now Hadoop is the predominant big data platform. There are many resources that describe Hadoop in great detail; here you will find a brief synopsis of many components and pointers on where to learn more.

Hadoop consists of three primary resources:

- The Hadoop Distributed File System (HDFS)
- The MapReduce programing platform
- The Hadoop ecosystem, a collection of tools that use or sit beside MapReduce and HDFS to store and organize data, and manage the machines that run Hadoop

These machines are called a *cluster*—a group of servers, almost always running some variant of the Linux operating system—that work together to perform a task.

The Hadoop ecosystem consists of modules that help program the system, manage and configure the cluster, manage data in the cluster, manage storage in the cluster, perform analytic tasks, and the like. The majority of the modules in this book will describe the components of the ecosystem and related technologies.

Hadoop Distributed File System (HDFS)

License	Apache License, Version 2.0
Activity	High
Purpose	High capacity, fault tolerant, inexpensive storage of very large datasets
Official Page	*http://hadoop.apache.org/docs/current/hadoop-project-dist/hadoop-hdfs/HdfsUserGuide.html*
Hadoop Integration	Fully Integrated

The Hadoop Distributed File System (HDFS) is the place in a Hadoop cluster where you store data. Built for data-intensive applications, the HDFS is designed to run on clusters of inexpensive commodity servers. HDFS is optimized for high-performance, read-intensive operations, and is resilient to failures in the cluster. It does not prevent failures, but is unlikely to lose data, because HDFS by default makes multiple copies of each of its data blocks. Moreover, HDFS is a write once, read many (or WORM-ish) filesystem: once a file is created, the filesystem API only allows you to append to the file, not to overwrite it. As a result, HDFS is usually inappropriate for normal online transaction processing (OLTP) applications. Most uses of HDFS are for sequential reads of large files. These files are broken into large blocks, usually 64 MB or larger in size, and these blocks are distributed among the nodes in the server.

HDFS is not a POSIX-compliant filesystem as you would see on Linux, Mac OS X, and on some Windows platforms (see the POSIX Wikipedia page (*http://bit.ly/16TI2GO*) for a brief explanation). It is not managed by the OS kernels on the nodes in the server. Blocks in HDFS are mapped to files in the host's underlying filesystem, often ext3 in Linux systems. HDFS does not assume that the underlying disks in the host are RAID protected, so by default, three copies of each block are made and are placed on different nodes in the cluster. This provides protection against lost data when nodes or disks fail and assists in Hadoop's notion of accessing data where it resides, rather than moving it through a network to access it.

Although an explanation is beyond the scope of this book, metadata about the files in the HDFS is managed through a NameNode, the Hadoop equivalent of the Unix/Linux superblock.

Tutorial Links

Oftentimes you'll be interacting with HDFS through other tools like Hive (described on page 34) or Pig (described on page 76). That said, there will be times when you want to work directly with HDFS; Yahoo! has published an excellent guide (*http://yhoo.it/1uEUNQJ*) for configuring and exploring a basic system.

Example Code

When you use the command-line interface (CLI) from a Hadoop client, you can copy a file from your local filesystem to the HDFS and then look at the first 10 lines with the following code snippet:

```
[hadoop@client-host ~]$ hadoop fs -ls /data
Found 4 items
drwxr-xr-x - hadoop supergroup 0 2012-07-12 08:55 /data/faa
-rw-r--r-- 1 hadoop supergroup 100 2012-08-02 13:29
/data/sample.txt
drwxr-xr-x - hadoop supergroup 0 2012-08-09 19:19 /data/wc
drwxr-xr-x - hadoop supergroup 0 2012-09-11 11:14 /data/weblogs

[hadoop@client-host ~]$ hadoop fs -ls /data/weblogs/

[hadoop@client-host ~]$ hadoop fs -mkdir /data/weblogs/in

[hadoop@client-host ~]$ hadoop fs -copyFromLocal
weblogs_Aug_2008.ORIG /data/weblogs/in

[hadoop@client-host ~]$ hadoop fs -ls /data/weblogs/in
Found 1 items
-rw-r--r-- 1 hadoop supergroup 9000 2012-09-11 11:15
/data/weblogs/in/weblogs_Aug_2008.ORIG

[hadoop@client-host ~]$ hadoop fs -cat
/data/weblogs/in/weblogs_Aug_2008.ORIG \
| head
10.254.0.51 - - [29/Aug/2008:12:29:13 -0700] "GGGG / HTTP/1.1"
200 1456
10.254.0.52 - - [29/Aug/2008:12:29:13 -0700] "GET / HTTP/1.1"
200 1456
10.254.0.53 - - [29/Aug/2008:12:29:13 -0700] "GET /apache_pb.gif
HTTP/1.1" 200 2326
10.254.0.54 - - [29/Aug/2008:12:29:13 -0700] "GET /favicon.ico
```

```
HTTP/1.1" 404 209
10.254.0.55 - - [29/Aug/2008:12:29:16 -0700] "GET /favicon.ico
HTTP/1.1"
404 209
10.254.0.56 - - [29/Aug/2008:12:29:21 -0700] "GET /mapreduce
HTTP/1.1" 301 236
10.254.0.57 - - [29/Aug/2008:12:29:21 -0700] "GET /develop/
HTTP/1.1" 200 2657
10.254.0.58 - - [29/Aug/2008:12:29:21 -0700] "GET
/develop/images/gradient.jpg
HTTP/1.1" 200 16624
10.254.0.59 - - [29/Aug/2008:12:29:27 -0700] "GET /manual/
HTTP/1.1" 200 7559
10.254.0.62 - - [29/Aug/2008:12:29:27 -0700] "GET
/manual/style/css/manual.css
HTTP/1.1" 200 18674
```

MapReduce

License	Apache License, Version 2.0
Activity	High
Purpose	A programming paradigm for processing big data
Official Page	*https://hadoop.apache.org*
Hadoop Integration	Fully Integrated

MapReduce was the first and is the primary programming framework for developing applications in Hadoop. You'll need to work in Java to use MapReduce in its original and pure form. You should study WordCount, the "Hello, world" program of Hadoop. The code comes with all the standard Hadoop distributions. Here's your problem in WordCount: you have a dataset that consists of a large set of documents, and the goal is to produce a list of all the words and the number of times they appear in the dataset.

MapReduce jobs consist of Java programs called *mappers* and *reducers*. Orchestrated by the Hadoop software, each of the mappers is given chunks of data to analyze. Let's assume it gets a sentence: "The dog ate the food." It would emit five name-value pairs or maps: "the":1, "dog":1, "ate":1, "the":1, and "food":1. The name in the name-value pair is the word, and the value is a count of how many times it appears. Hadoop takes the result of your map job and sorts it. For each map, a hash value is created to assign it to a reducer in a step called the shuffle. The reducer would sum all the maps for each word in its input stream and produce a sorted list of words in the document. You can think of mappers as programs that extract data from HDFS files into maps, and reducers as programs that take the output from the mappers and aggregate results. The tutorials linked in the following section explain this in greater detail.

You'll be pleased to know that much of the hard work—dividing up the input datasets, assigning the mappers and reducers to nodes, shuffling the data from the mappers to the reducers, and writing out the final results to the HDFS—is managed by Hadoop itself. Programmers merely have to write the map and reduce functions. Mappers and reducers are usually written in Java (as in the example cited at the conclusion of this section), and writing MapReduce code is nontrivial for novices. To that end, higher-level constructs have been developed to do this. Pig is one example and will be discussed on page 76. Hadoop Streaming is another.

Tutorial Links

There are a number of excellent tutorials for working with MapReduce. A good place to start is the official Apache documentation (*http://bit.ly/1KMvKgv*), but Yahoo! has also put together a tutorial module (*http://yhoo.it/1MEF6ie*). The folks at MapR, a commercial software company that makes a Hadoop distribution, have a great presentation (*http://youtu.be/kM76O4cZ5_0*) on writing MapReduce.

Example Code

Writing MapReduce can be fairly complicated and is beyond the scope of this book. A typical application that folks write to get started is a simple word count. The official documentation includes a tutorial (*http://bit.ly/1yhaB7q*) for building that application.

YARN

License	Apache License, Version 2.0
Activity	Medium
Purpose	Processing
Official Page	*https://hadoop.apache.org/docs/current/hadoop-yarn/hadoop-yarn-site/YARN.html*
Hadoop Integration	Fully Integrated

When many folks think about Hadoop, they are really thinking about two related technologies. These two technologies are the Hadoop Distributed File System (HDFS), which houses your data, and MapReduce, which allows you to actually do things with your data. While MapReduce is great for certain categories of tasks, it falls short with others. This led to fracturing in the ecosystem and a variety of tools that live outside of your Hadoop cluster but attempt to communicate with HDFS.

In May 2012, version 2.0 of Hadoop was released, and with it came an exciting change to the way you can interact with your data. This change came with the introduction of YARN, which stands for Yet Another Resource Negotiator.

YARN exists in the space between your data and where MapReduce now lives, and it allows for many other tools that used to live outside your Hadoop system, such as Spark and Giraph, to now exist natively within a Hadoop cluster. It's important to understand that Yarn does not replace MapReduce; in fact, Yarn doesn't do anything at all on its own. What Yarn does do is provide a convenient, uniform way for a variety of tools such as MapReduce, HBase, or any custom utilities you might build to run on your Hadoop cluster.

Tutorial Links

YARN is still an evolving technology, and the official Apache guide (*http://bit.ly/1E9z6ry*) is really the best place to get started.

Example Code

The truth is that writing applications in Yarn is still very involved and too deep for this book. You can find a link to an excellent walk-through for building your first Yarn application in the preceding "Tutorial Links" section.

Spark

License	Apache License, Version 2.0
Activity	High
Purpose	Processing/Storage
Official Page	*http://spark.apache.org/*
Hadoop Integration	API Compatible

MapReduce is the primary workhorse at the core of most Hadoop clusters. While highly effective for very large batch-analytic jobs, MapReduce has proven to be suboptimal for applications like graph analysis that require iterative processing and data sharing.

Spark is designed to provide a more flexible model that supports many of the multipass applications that falter in MapReduce. It accomplishes this goal by taking advantage of memory whenever possible in order to reduce the amount of data that is written to and read from disk. Unlike Pig and Hive, Spark is not a tool for making MapReduce easier to use. It is a complete replacement for MapReduce that includes its own work execution engine.

Spark operates with three core ideas:

Resilient Distributed Dataset (RDD)
RDDs contain data that you want to transform or analyze. They can either be be read from an external source, such as a file or a database, or they can be created by a transformation.

Transformation
A transformation modifies an existing RDD to create a new RDD. For example, a filter that pulls ERROR messages out of a log file would be a transformation.

Action

> An action analyzes an RDD and returns a single result. For example, an action would count the number of results identified by our ERROR filter.

If you want to do any significant work in Spark, you would be wise to learn about Scala, a functional programming language. Scala (*http://www.scala-lang.org*) combines object orientation with functional programming. Because Lisp is an older functional programming language, Scala might be called "Lisp joins the 21st century." This is not to say that Scala is the only way to work with Spark. The project also has strong support for Java and Python, but when new APIs or features are added, they appear first in Scala.

Tutorial Links

A quick start (*http://bit.ly/1upkhfx*) for Spark can be found on the project home page.

Example Code

We'll start with opening the Spark shell by running *./bin/spark-shell* from the directory we installed Spark in.

In this example, we're going to count the number of *Dune* reviews in our review file:

```
// Read the csv file containing our reviews
scala> val reviews = spark.textFile("hdfs://reviews.csv")
testFile: spark.RDD[String] = spark.MappedRDD@3d7e837f

// This is a two-part operation:
// first we'll filter down to the two
// lines that contain Dune reviews
// then we'll count those lines
scala> val dune_reviews = reviews.filter(line =>
  line.contains("Dune")).count()
res0: Long = 2
```

CHAPTER 2

Database and Data Management

If you're planning to use Hadoop, it's likely that you'll be managing lots of data, and in addition to MapReduce jobs, you may need some kind of database. Since the advent of Google's BigTable, Hadoop has an interest in the management of data. While there are some relational SQL databases or SQL interfaces to HDFS data, like Hive, much data management in Hadoop uses non-SQL techniques to store and access data. The NoSQL Archive (*http://nosql-database.org/*) lists more than 150 NoSQL databases that are then classified as:

- Column stores
- Document stores
- Key-value/tuple stores
- Graph databases
- Multimodel databases
- Object databases
- Grid and cloud databases
- Multivalue databases
- Tabular stores
- Others

NoSQL databases generally do not support relational join operations, complex transactions, or foreign-key constraints common in relational systems but generally scale better to large amounts of data.

You'll have to decide what works best for your datasets and the information you wish to extract from them. It's quite possible that you'll be using more than one.

This book will look at many of the leading examples in each section, but the focus will be on the two major categories: key-value stores and document stores (illustrated in Figure 2-1).

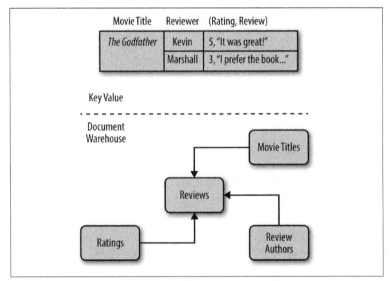

Figure 2-1. Two approaches to indexing

A key-value store can be thought of like a catalog. All the items in a catalog (the values) are organized around some sort of index (the keys). Just like a catalog, a key-value store is very quick and effective if you know the key you're looking for, but isn't a whole lot of help if you don't.

For example, let's say I'm looking for Marshall's review of *The Godfather*. I can quickly refer to my index, find all the reviews for that film, and scroll down to Marshall's review: "I prefer the book…"

A document warehouse, on the other hand, is a much more flexible type of database. Rather than forcing you to organize your data around a specific key, it allows you to index and search for your data based on any number of parameters. Let's expand on the last example and say I'm in the mood to watch a movie based on a book. One naive way to find such a movie would be to search for reviews that contain the word "book."

In this case, a key-value store wouldn't be a whole lot of help, as my key is not very clearly defined. What I need is a document warehouse that will let me quickly search all the text of all the reviews and find those that contain the word "book."

Cassandra

License	GPL v2
Activity	High
Purpose	Key-value store
Official Page	*https://cassandra.apache.org*
Hadoop Integration	API Compatible

Oftentimes you may need to simply organize some of your big data for easy retrieval. One common way to do this is to use a key-value datastore. This type of database looks like the white pages in a phone book. Your data is organized by a unique "key," and values are associated with that key. For example, if you want to store information about your customers, you may use their username as the key, and information such as transaction history and addresses as values associated with that key.

Key-value datastores are a common fixture in any big data system because they are easy to scale, quick, and straightforward to work with. Cassandra is a distributed key-value database designed with simplicity and scalability in mind. While often compared to HBase (described on page 19), Cassandra differs in a few key ways:

- Cassandra is an all-inclusive system, which means it does not require a Hadoop environment or any other big data tools.
- Cassandra is completely masterless: it operates as a peer-to-peer system. This makes it easier to configure and highly resilient.

Tutorial Links

DataStax, a company that provides commercial support for Cassandra, offers a set of freely available videos (*http://bit.ly/1DhUA7t*).

Example Code

The easiest way to interact with Cassandra is through its shell interface. You start the shell by running *bin/cqlsh* from your install directory.

Then you need to create a keyspace. Keyspaces are similar to schemas in traditional relational databases; they are a convenient way to organize your tables. A typical pattern is to use a single different keyspace for each application:

```
CREATE KEYSPACE field_guide
WITH REPLICATION = {
    'class': 'SimpleStrategy', 'replication factor' : 3 };

USE field_guide;
```

Now that you have a keyspace, you'll create a table within that keyspace to hold your reviews. This table will have three columns and a primary key that consists of both the reviewer and the title, as that pair should be unique within the database:

```
CREATE TABLE reviews (
    reviewer varchar,
    title varchar,
    rating int,
    PRIMARY KEY (reviewer, title));
```

Once your table is created, you can insert a few reviews:

```
INSERT INTO reviews (reviewer,title,rating)
    VALUES ('Kevin','Dune',10);
INSERT INTO reviews (reviewer,title,rating)
    VALUES ('Marshall','Dune',1);
INSERT INTO reviews (reviewer,title,rating)
    VALUES ('Kevin','Casablanca',5);
```

And now that you have some data, you will create an index that will allow you to execute a simple SQL query to retrieve *Dune* reviews:

```
CREATE INDEX ON reviews (title);

SELECT * FROM reviews WHERE title = 'Dune';

 reviewer |       title | rating
----------+------------+-------
    Kevin |       Dune |     10
 Marshall |       Dune |      1
    Kevin | Casablanca |      5
```

HBase

License	Apache License, Version 2.0
Activity	High
Purpose	NoSQL database with random access
Official Page	*https://hbase.apache.org*
Hadoop Integration	Fully Integrated

There are many situations in which you might have sparse data. That is, there are many attributes of the data, but each observation only has a few of them. For example, you might want a table of various tickets in a help-desk application. Tickets for email might have different information (and attributes or columns) than tickets for network problems or lost passwords, or issues with backup system. There are other situations in which you have data that has a large number of common values in a column or attribute, say "country" or "state." Each of these example might lead you to consider HBase.

HBase is a NoSQL database system included in the standard Hadoop distributions. It is a key-value store, logically. This means that rows are defined by a key, and have associated with them a number of bins (or columns) where the associated values are stored. The only data type is the byte string. Physically, groups of similar columns are stored together in column families. Most often, HBase is accessed via Java code, but APIs exist for using HBase with Pig, Thrift, Jython (Python based), and others. HBase is not normally accessed in a MapReduce fashion. It does have a shell interface for interactive use.

HBase is often used for applications that may require sparse rows. That is, each row may use only a few of the defined columns. It is fast (as Hadoop goes) when access to elements is done through the primary key, or defining key value. It's highly scalable and reasonably fast. Unlike traditional HDFS applications, it permits random access to rows, rather than sequential searches.

Though faster than MapReduce, you should not use HBase for any kind of transactional needs, nor any kind of relational analytics. It does not support any secondary indexes, so finding all rows where a given column has a specific value is tedious and must be done at the application level. HBase does not have a JOIN operation; this must be done by the individual application. You must provide security at the application level; other tools like Accumulo (described on page 22) are built with security in mind.

While Cassandra (described on page 16) and MongoDB (described on page 31) might still be the predominant NoSQL databases today, HBase is gaining in popularity and may well be the leader in the near future.

Tutorial Links

The folks at Coreservlets.com have put together a handful of Hadoop tutorials including an excellent series on HBase (*http://bit.ly/1zWjIhF*). There's also a handful of video tutorials available on the Internet, including this one (*http://youtu.be/IumVWII3fRQ*), which we found particularly helpful.

Example Code

In this example, your goal is to find the average review for the movie *Dune*. Each movie review has three elements: a reviewer name, a film title, and a rating (an integer from 0 to 10). The example is done in the HBase shell:

```
hbase(main):008:0> create 'reviews', 'cf1'
0 row(s) in 1.0710 seconds

hbase(main):013:0> put 'reviews', 'dune-marshall', \
hbase(main):014:0> 'cf1:score', 1
0 row(s) in 0.0370 seconds

hbase(main):015:0> put 'reviews', 'dune-kevin', \
hbase(main):016:0> 'cf1:score', 10
0 row(s) in 0.0090 seconds

hbase(main):017:0> put 'reviews', 'casablanca-kevin', \
hbase(main):018:0> 'cf1:score', 5
0 row(s) in 0.0130 seconds
```

```
hbase(main):019:0> put 'reviews', 'blazingsaddles-bob', \
hbase(main):020:0> 'cf1:score', 9
0 row(s) in 0.0090 seconds

hbase(main):021:0> scan 'reviews'
ROW                        COLUMN+CELL
 blazingsaddles-bob        column=cf1:score,
                           timestamp=1390598651108,
                           value=9
 casablanca-kevin          column=cf1:score,
                           timestamp=1390598627889,
                           value=5
 dune-kevin                column=cf1:score,
                           timestamp=1390598600034,
                           value=10
 dune-marshall             column=cf1:score,
                           timestamp=1390598579439,
                           value=1
3 row(s) in 0.0290 seconds

hbase(main):024:0> scan 'reviews', {STARTROW => 'dune', \
hbase(main):025:0> ENDROW => 'dunf'}
ROW                        COLUMN+CELL
 dune-kevin                column=cf1:score,
                           timestamp=1390598791384,
                           value=10
 dune-marshall             column=cf1:score,
                           timestamp=1390598579439,
                           value=1
2 row(s) in 0.0090 seconds
```

Now you've retrieved the two rows using an efficient range scan, but how do you compute the average? In the HBase shell, it's not possible; using the HBase Java APIs, you can extract the values, but there is no built-in row aggregation function for average or sum, so you would need to do this in your Java code.

The choice of the row key is critical in HBase. If you want to find the average rating of all the movies Kevin has reviewed, you would need to do a full table scan, potentially a very tedious task with a very large dataset. You might want to have two versions of the table, one with the row key given by reviewer-film and another with film-reviewer. Then you would have the problem of ensuring they're in sync.

Accumulo

License	Apache License, Version 2.0
Activity	High
Purpose	Name-value database with cell-level security
Official Page	*http://accumulo.apache.org/index.html*
Hadoop Integration	Fully Integrated

You have an application that could use a good column/name-value store, like HBase (described on page 19), but you have an additional security issue; you must carefully control which users can see which cells in your data. For example, you could have a multitenancy data store in which you are storing data from different divisions in your enterprise in a single table and want to ensure that users from one division cannot see the data from another, but that senior management can see across the whole enterprise. For internal security reasons, the U.S. National Security Agency (NSA) developed Accumulo and then donated the code to the Apache foundation.

You might notice a great deal of similarity between HBase and Accumulo, as both systems are modeled on Google's BigTable. Accumulo improves on that model with its focus on security and cell-based access control. Each user has a set of security labels, simple text strings. Suppose yours were "admin," "audit," and "GroupW." When you want to define the access to a particular cell, you set the column visibility for that column in a given row to a Boolean expression of the various labels. In this syntax, the & is logical AND and | is logical OR. If the cell's visibility rule were admin|audit, then any user with either admin or audit label could see that cell. If the column visibility rule were admin&Group7, you would not be able to see it, as you lack the Group7 label, and both are required.

But Accumulo is more than just security. It also can run at massive scale, with many petabytes of data with hundreds of thousands of ingest and retrieval operations per second.

Tutorial Links

For more information on Accumulo, check out the following resources:

- An introduction (*http://slidesha.re/1E9zxlK*) from Aaron Cordova, one of the originators of Accumulo.
- A video tutorial (*http://youtu.be/5RPaDzOwqQ8*) that focuses on performance and the Accumulo architecture.
- This tutorial (*http://youtu.be/71J65mKm6ZU*) is more focused on security and encryption.
- The 2014 Accumulo Summit (*http://bit.ly/1zvSXwT*) has a wealth of information.

Example Code

Good example code is a bit long and complex to include here, but can be found on the "Examples" section (*http://bit.ly/16TINzP*) of the project's home page.

Memcached

License	Revised BSD License
Activity	Medium
Purpose	In-Memory Cache
Official Page	*http://memcached.org*
Hadoop Integration	No Integration

It's entirely likely you will eventually encounter a situation where you need very fast access to a large amount of data for a short period of time. For example, let's say you want to send an email to your customers and prospects letting them know about new features you've added to your product, but you also need to make certain you exclude folks you've already contacted this month.

The way you'd typically address this query in a big data system is by distributing your large contact list across many machines, and then loading the entirety of your list of folks contacted this month into memory on each machine and quickly checking each contact against your list of those you've already emailed. In MapReduce, this is often referred to as a "replicated join." However, let's assume you've got a large network of contacts consisting of many millions of email addresses you've collected from trade shows, product demos, and social media, and you like to contact these people fairly often. This means your list of folks you've already contacted this month could be fairly large and the entire list might not fit into the amount of memory you've got available on each machine.

What you really need is some way to pool memory across all your machines and let everyone refer back to that large pool. Memcached is a tool that lets you build such a distributed memory pool. To follow up on our previous example, you would store the entire list of folks who've already been emailed into your distributed memory pool and instruct all the different machines processing your full contact list to refer back to that memory pool instead of local memory.

Tutorial Links

The spymemcached project (*http://bit.ly/1zLRaZC*) has a handful of examples using its API available on its wiki (*http://bit.ly/1KMwgv8*).

Example Code

Let's say we need to keep track of which reviewers have already reviewed which movies, so we don't ask a reviewer to review the same movie twice. Because there is no single, officially supported Java client for Memcached, we'll use the popular spymemcached client.

We'll start by defining a client and pointing it at our Memcached servers:

```
MemcachedClient client = new MemcachedClient(
    AddrUtil.getAddresses("server1:11211 server2:11211"));
```

Now we'll start loading data into our cache. We'll use the popular OpenCSV library (*http://opencsv.sourceforge.net*) to read our reviews file and write an entry to our cache for every reviewer and title pair we find:

```
CSVReader reader = new CSVReader(new FileReader("reviews.csv"));
String [] line;
while ((line = reader.readNext()) != null) {
    //Merge the reviewer name and the movie title
    //into a single value (ie: KevinDune)
    //that we'll use as a key
    String reviewerAndTitle = line[0] + line[1];
    //Write the key to our cache and store it for 30 minutes
    //(188 seconds)
    client.set(reviewerAndTitle, 1800, true);
}
```

Once we have our values loaded into the cache, we can quickly check the cache from a MapReduce job or any other Java code:

```
Object myObject=client.get(aKey);
```

Blur

License	Apache License, Version 2.0
Activity	Medium
Purpose	Document Warehouse
Official Page	*https://incubator.apache.org/blur*
Hadoop Integration	Fully Integrated

Let's say you've bought in to the entire big data story using Hadoop. You've got Flume gathering data and pushing it into HDFS, your MapReduce jobs are transforming that data and building key-value pairs that are pushed into HBase, and you even have a couple enterprising data scientists using Mahout to analyze your data. At this point, your CTO walks up to you and asks how often one of your specific products is mentioned in a feedback form your are collecting from your users. Your heart drops as you realize the feedback is free-form text and you've got no way to search any of that data.

Blur is a tool for indexing and searching text with Hadoop. Because it has Lucene (a very popular text-indexing framework) at its core, it has many useful features, including fuzzy matching, wildcard searches, and paged results. It allows you to search through unstructured data in a way that would otherwise be very difficult.

Tutorial Links

You can't go wrong with the official "getting started" guide on the project home page (*http://bit.ly/1CgXgRf*). There is also an excellent, though slightly out of date, presentation (*http://youtu.be/ w4zLz9ussdI*) from a Hadoop User Group meeting in 2011.

Example Code

There are a couple different ways to load data into Blur. When you have large amounts of data you want to index in bulk, you will likely use MapReduce, whereas if you want to stream data in, you are likely better off with the mutation interface. In this case, we're going to use the mutation interface, as we're just going to index a couple records:

```
import static org.apache.blur.thrift.util.BlurThriftHelper.*;

Iface aClient = BlurClient.getClient(
    "controller1:40010,controller2:40010");

//Create a new Row in table 1
RowMutation mutation1 = newRowMutation("reviews", "Dune",
    newRecordMutation("review", "review_1.json",
        newColumn("Reviewer", "Kevin"),
        newColumn("Rating", "10")
        newColumn(
            "Text",
            "I was taken away with the movie's greatness!")
    ),
    newRecordMutation("review", "review_2.json",
        newColumn("Reviewer", "Marshall"),
        newColumn("Rating", "1")
        newColumn(
            "Text",
            "I thought the movie was pretty terrible :(")
    )
);

client.mutate(mutation);
```

Now let's say we want to search for all reviews where the review text mentions something being great. We're going to pull up the Blur shell by running */bin/blur shell* from our installation directory and run a simple query. This query tells Blur to look in the "Text" column of the review column family in the reviews table for anything that looks like the word "great":

```
blur> query reviews review.Text:great
  - Results Summary -
    total : 1
    time : 41.372 ms
-------------------------------------------------------------
    hit : 0
    score : 0.9548232184568715
```

```
      id : Dune
recordId : review_1.json
  family : review
    Text : I was taken away with the movie's greatness!
----------------------------------------------------------------
- Results Summary -
   total : 1
   time  : 41.372 ms
```

Solr

License	Apache License, Version 2.0
Activity	High
Purpose	Document Warehouse
Official Page	*https://lucene.apache.org/solr*
Hadoop Integration	API Compatible

Sometimes you just want to search through a big stack of documents. Not all tasks require big, complex analysis jobs spanning petabytes of data. For many common use cases, you may find that you have too much data for a simple Unix grep or Windows search, but not quite enough to warrant a team of data scientists. Solr fits comfortably in that middle ground, providing an easy-to-use means to quickly index and search the contents of many documents.

Solr supports a distributed architecture that provides many of the benefits you expect from big data systems (e.g., linear scalability, data replication, and failover). It is based on Lucene, a popular framework for indexing and searching documents, and implements that framework by providing a set of tools for building indexes and querying data.

While Solr is able to use the Hadoop Distributed File System (HDFS; described on page 3) to store data, it is not truly compatible with Hadoop and does not use MapReduce (described on page 6) or YARN (described on page 8) to build indexes or respond to queries. There is a similar effort named Blur (described on page 26) to build a tool on top of the Lucene framework that leverages the entire Hadoop stack.

Tutorial Links

Apart from the tutorial on the official Solr home page, there is a Solr wiki (*http://bit.ly/199s7Wh*) with great information.

Example Code

In this example, we're going to assume we have a set of semi-structured data consisting of movie reviews with labels that clearly mark the title and the text of the review. These reviews will be stored in individual JSON files in the *reviews* directory.

We'll start by telling Solr to index our data; there are a handful of different ways to do this, all with unique trade-offs. In this case, we're going to use the simplest mechanism, which is the *post.sh* script located in the *exampledocs/* subdirectory of our Solr install:

```
./example/exampledocs/post.sh /reviews/*.json
```

Once our reviews have been indexed, they are ready to search. Solr has its own graphical user interface (GUI) that can be used for simple searches. We'll pull up that GUI and search for movie reviews that contain the word "great":

```
review_text:great&fl=title
```

This search tells Solr that we want to retrieve the `title` field (`fl=title`) for any review where the word "great" appears in the `review_text` field.

MongoDB

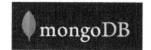

License	Free Software Foundation's GNU AGPL v3.0.; commercial licenses available from MongoDB, Inc.
Activity	High
Purpose	JSON document-oriented database
Official Page	*http://www.mongodb.org*
Hadoop Integration	API Compatible

If you have a large number of JSON documents (described on page 48) in your Hadoop cluster and need some data management tool to effectively use them, consider MongoDB, an open source, big data, document-oriented database whose documents are JSON objects. At the start of 2015, it is one of the most popular NoSQL databases. Unlike some other database systems, MongoDB supports secondary indexes—meaning it is possible to quickly search on other than the primary key that uniquely identifies each document in the Mongo database. The name derives from the slang word "humongous," meaning very, very large. While MongoDB did not originally run on Hadoop and the HDFS, it can be used in conjunction with Hadoop.

MongoDB is a document-oriented database, the document being a JSON object. In relational databases, you have tables and rows. In MongoDB, the equivalent of a row is a JSON document, and the analog to a table is a collection, a set of JSON documents. To understand MongoDB, you should skip ahead to "JSON" on page 48 of this book.

Perhaps the best way to understand its use is by way of a code example, shown in the next "Example Code" section.

Tutorial Links

The tutorials section (*http://bit.ly/1zWkb3B*) on the official project page is a great place to get started. There are also plenty of videos available on the Internet, including this informative series (*http://youtu.be/liQzIsFnCr0*).

Example Code

This time you'll want to compute the average ranking of the movie *Dune* in the standard dataset. If you know Python, this will be clear. If you don't, the code is still pretty straightforward:

```
#!/usr/bin/python
# import required packages
import sys
import pymongo

# json movie reviews
movieReviews = [
    { "reviewer":"Kevin", "movie":"Dune", "rating","10" },
    { "reviewer":"Marshall", "movie":"Dune", "rating","1" },
    { "reviewer":"Kevin", "movie":"Casablanca", "rating","5" },
    { "reviewer":"Bob", "movie":"Blazing Saddles", "rating","9" }
]

# MongoDB connection info
MONGODB_INFO = 'mongodb://juser:password@localhost:27018/db'

# connect to MongoDB
client=pymongo.MongoClient(MONGODB_INFO)
db=client.get_defalut_database()

# create the movies collection
movies=db['movies']

#insert the movie reviews
movies.insert(movieReviews)

# find all the movies with title Dune, iterate through them
# finding all scores by using
# standard db cursor technology
mcur=movies.find({'movie': {'movie': 'Dune'})
count=0
sum=0

# for all reviews of Dune, count them up and sum the rankings
for m in mcur:
    count += 1
```

```
    sum += m['rating']
client.close()
rank=float(sum)/float(count)
print ('Dune %s\n' % rank)
```

Hive

License	Apache License, Version 2.0
Activity	High
Purpose	Data Interaction
Official Page	*http://hive.apache.org*
Integration	Fully Integrated

At first, all access to data in your Hadoop cluster came through MapReduce jobs written in Java. This worked fine during Hadoop's infancy when all Hadoop users had a stable of Java-savvy coders. However, as Hadoop emerged into the broader world, many wanted to adopt Hadoop but had stables of SQL coders for whom writing MapReduce would be a steep learning curve. Enter Hive. The goal of Hive is to allow SQL access to data in the HDFS. The Apache Hive data-warehouse software facilitates querying and managing large datasets residing in HDFS. Hive defines a simple SQL-like query language, called HQL, that enables users familiar with SQL to query the data. Queries written in HQL are converted into MapReduce code by Hive and executed by Hadoop. But beware! HQL is not full ANSI-standard SQL. While the basics are covered, some features are missing. Here's a partial list as of early 2015:

- Hive does not support non-equality join conditions.
- Update and delete statements are not supported.
- Transactions are not supported.

You may not need these, but if you run code generated by third-party solutions, they may generate non-Hive compliant code.

Hive does not mandate read or written data be in the "Hive format" —there is no such thing. This means your data can be accessed directly by Hive without any of the extract, transform, and load (ETL) preprocessing typically required by traditional relational databases.

Tutorial Links

A couple of great resources are the official Hive tutorial (*http://bit.ly/1KJbmih*) and this video (*http://youtu.be/Pn7Sp2-hUXE*) published by the folks at HortonWorks.

Example Code

Say we have a comma-separated values (CSV) file containing movie reviews with information about the reviewer, the movie, and the rating:

```
Kevin,Dune,10
Marshall,Dune,1
Kevin,Casablanca,5
Bob,Blazing Saddles,9
```

First, we need to define the schema for our data:

```
CREATE TABLE movie_reviews
    ( reviewer STRING, title STRING, rating INT)
ROW FORMAT DELIMITED
FILEDS TERMINATED BY '\,'
STORED AS TEXTFILE
```

Next, we need to load the data by pointing the table at our movie reviews file. Because Hive doesn't require that data be stored in any specific format, loading a table consists simply of pointing Hive at a file in HDFS:

```
LOAD DATA LOCAL INPATH 'reviews.csv'
OVERWRITE INTO TABLE movie_reviews
```

Now we are ready to perform some sort of analysis. Let's say, in this case, we want to find the average rating for the movie *Dune*:

```
Select AVG(rating) FROM movie_reviews WHERE title = 'Dune';
```

Spark SQL (formerly Shark)

License	Apache License, Version 2.0
Activity	High
Purpose	SQL access to Hadoop Data
Official Page	*http://spark.apache.org/sql/*
Hadoop Integration	API Compatible

If you need SQL access to your data, and Hive (described on page 34) is a bit underperforming, and you're willing to commit to a Spark environment (described on page 10), then you need to consider Spark SQL. SQL access in Spark was originally called the Shark project, and was a port of Hive, but Shark has ceased development and its successor, Spark SQL, is now the mainline SQL project on Spark. The blog post "Shark, Spark SQL, Hive on Spark, and the Future of SQL on Spark" (*http://bit.ly/1AmBixa*) provides more information about the change. Spark SQL, like Spark, has an in-memory computing model, which helps to account for its speed. It's only in recent years that decreasing memory costs have made large memory Linux servers ubiquitous, thus leading to recent advances in in-memory computing for large datasets. Because memory access times are usually 100 times as fast as disk access times, it's quite appealing to keep as much in memory as possible, using the disks as infrequently as possible. But abandoning MapReduce has made Spark SQL much faster, even if it requires disk access.

While Spark SQL speaks HQL, the Hive query language, it has a few extra features that aren't in Hive. One is the ability to encache table data for the duration of a user session. This corresponds to temporary tables in many other databases, but unlike other databases, these tables live in memory and are thus accessed much faster. Spark

SQL also allows access to tables as though they were Spark Resilient Distributed Datasets (RDD).

Spark SQL supports the Hive metastore, most of its query language, and data formats, so existing Hive users should have an easier time converting to Shark than many others. However, while the Spark SQL documentation is currently not absolutely clear on this, not all the Hive features have yet been implemented in Spark SQL. APIs currently exist for Python, Java, and Scala. See "Hive" on page 34 for more details. Spark SQL also can run Spark's MLlib machine-learning algorithms as SQL statements.

Spark SQL can use JSON (described on page 48) and Parquet (described on page 52) as data sources, so it's pretty useful in an HDFS environment.

Tutorial Links

There are a wealth of tutorials on the project home page (*http:// bit.ly/1E9AmLj*).

Example Code

At the user level, Shark looks like Hive, so if you can code in Hive, you can almost code in Spark SQL. But you need to set up your Spark SQL environment. Here's how you would do it in Python using the movie review data we use in other examples (to understand the setup, you'll need to read "Spark" on page 10, as well as have some knowledge of Python):

```
# Spark requires a Context object.  Let's assume it exists
# already. You need a SQL Context object as well
from pyspark.sql import SQLContext
sqlContext = SQLContext(sc)

# Load a the CSV text file and convert each line to a Python
# dictionary using lambda notation for anonymous functions.
lines = sc.textFile("reviews.csv")
movies = lines.map(lambda l: l.split(","))
reviews = movies.map(
    lambda p: {"name": p[0], "title": p[1], "rating": int(p[2])})

# Spark SQL needs to think of the RDD
# (Resilient Distributed Dataset) as a data schema
# and register the table name
schemaReviews = sqlContext.inferSchema(reviews)
schemaReviews.registerAsTable("reviews")
```

```
# once you've registered the RDD as a schema,
# you can run SQL statements over it.
dune_reviews = sqlContext.sql(
    "SELECT * FROM reviews WHERE title = 'Dune'")
```

Giraph

License	Apache License, Version 2.0
Activity	High
Purpose	Graph database
Official Page	*https://giraph.apache.org*
Hadoop Integration	Fully Integrated

You may know a parlor game called Six Degrees of Separation from Kevin Bacon in which movie trivia experts try to find the closest relationship between a movie actor and Kevin Bacon. If an actor is in the same movie, that's a "path" of length 1. If an actor has never been in a movie with Kevin Bacon, but has been in a movie with an actor who has been, that's a path of length 2. It rests on the assumption that any individual involved in the film industry can be linked through his or her film roles to Kevin Bacon within six steps, or six degrees of separation. For example, there is an arc between Kevin Bacon and Sean Penn, because they were both in *Mystic River*, so they have one degree of separation or a path of length 1. But Benicio Del Toro has a path of length 2 because he has never been in a movie with Kevin Bacon, but has been in one with Sean Penn.

You can show these relationships by means of a graph, a set of ordered pairs (N,M) which describe a connection from N to M.

You can think of a tree (such as a hierarchical filesystem) as a graph with a single source node or origin, and arcs leading down the tree branches. The set {(top, b1), (top, b2), (b1,c1), (b1,c2), (b2,c3)} is a tree rooted at top, with branches from top to b1 and b2, b1 to c1 and c2, and b2 to c3. The elements of the set {top, b1, b2, c1,c2,c3} are called the nodes.

You will find graphs useful in describing relationships between entities. For example, if you had a collection of emails sent between people in your organization, you could build a graph where each node represents a person in your organization and an arc would exist between node a and node b if a sent an email to b or vice versa. It could look like Figure 2-2.

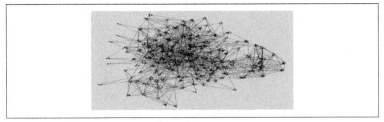

Figure 2-2. A graph detailing email relationships between people

Giraph is an Apache project to build and extract information from graphs. For example, you could use Giraph to calculate the shortest distance (number of arc hops) from one node in the graph to another or to calculate if there was a path between two nodes.

Apache Giraph is derived from a Google project called Pregel and has been used by Facebook to build and analyze a graph with a trillion nodes, admittedly on a very large Hadoop cluster. It is built using a technology called Bulk Synchronous Parallel (BSP).

The general notion is that there are a set of "supersteps" in the BSP model. In step zero, the vertices or nodes are distributed to worker processes. In each following superstep, each of the vertices iterates through a set of messages it received from the previous superset and sends messages to other nodes to which it is connected.

In the Kevin Bacon example, each node represents an actor, director, producer, screenwriter, and so on. Each arc connects two people who are part of the same movie. And we want to test the hypothesis that everyone in the industry is connected to Kevin Bacon within six hops in the graph. Each node is given an initial value to the number of hops; for Kevin Bacon, it is zero. For everyone else, the initial value is a very large integer. At the first superstep, each node sends its value to all those nodes connected to it. Then, at each of the other supersteps, each node first reads all its messages and takes the minimum value. If it is less than its current value, the node adds 1 and then sends this to all its connected nodes at the end of the superstep.

Why? Because if a connected node is N steps from Kevin, then this node is at mosts N+1 steps away. Once a node has established a new value, it opts out of sending more messages.

At the end of six supersteps, you'll have all the persons connected to Kevin Bacon by six or fewer hops.

Tutorial Links

The official product page has a quick start guide (*http://bit.ly/1vkfaxD*). In addition, there are a handful of videotaped talks, including one by PayPal (*http://youtu.be/_xha7OdEy2A*) and another by Facebook (*http://youtu.be/b5Qmz4zPj-M*). Finally, there's this particularly informative blog post (*http://bit.ly/1DhV1i3*).

## CHAPTER 3

Serialization

Big data systems spend a great deal of time and resources moving data around. Take, for example, a typical process that looks at logs. That process might collect logs from a few servers, moving those logs to HDFS, perform some sort of analysis to build a handful of reports, then move those reports to some sort of dashboard your users can see. At each step in that process, you're moving data, in some cases multiple times, between systems, off hard drives and into memory. See Figure 3-1.

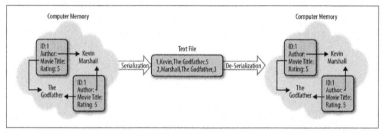

Figure 3-1. Serialization and deserialization of a movie review

When modern computers work with data, it's often held in all manner of complex formats, full of internal relationships and references. When you want to write this data down, whether to share it or to store it for later, you need to find a way to break down those relationships, explain the references, and build a representation of the data that can be read from start to finish. This process is called serialization.

Similarly, have you ever read a great description of a place or event and found that you could picture it perfectly in your head? This process of reading something that's been written down (serialized) and rebuilding all the complex references and relationships is known as de-serialization.

There is a wide variety of data serialization tools and frameworks available to help manage what your data looks like as it is moved around. Choosing the right serialization format for each task is a critical aspect of building a system that is scalable, performs well, and can be easily managed. As you'll see, there are a handful of major considerations to keep in mind when choosing a serialization format, including:

Data size
 How much space does your data take up in memory or on disk?

Read/write speed
 How long does it take a computer to read/write your data?

Human readability
 Can humans make sense out of your serialized data without outside assistance?

Ease of use
 How hard is it to write or read data in this format? Do you need to share special files or tools with other folks who want to read your data?

Avro

License	Apache License, Version 2.0
Activity	Medium
Purpose	Data Serialization
Official Page	*http://avro.apache.org*
Hadoop Integration	API Compatible

Let's say you have some data and you want to share it with someone else. The first thing you might do is write out the structure of your data, defining things like how many fields there are and what kind of data those fields contain. In technical terms, that definition could be called a *schema*. You would likely share that schema along with your data, and the folks who are interested in your data might put together a little code to make sure they can read it.

Avro is a system that automates much of that work. You provide it with a schema, and it builds the code you need to read and write data. Because Avro was designed from the start to work with Hadoop and big data, it goes to great lengths to store your data as efficiently as possible.

There are two unique behaviors that differentiate Avro from many other serialization systems such as Thrift and Protocol Buffers (protobuf; described on page 50):

Runtime assembled

Avro does not require special serialization code to be generated and shared beforehand. This simplifies the process of deploying applications that span multiple platforms, but comes at a cost to performance. In some cases, you can work around this and generate the code beforehand, but you'll need to regenerate and reshare the code every time you change the format of your data.

Schema-driven

Each data transfer consists of two parts: a schema describing the format of the data and the data itself. Because the format of the data is defined in the schema, each item does not need to be tagged. This allows for a dramatic reduction in the overhead associated with transferring many complex objects, but can actually increase the overhead involved with transferring a small number of large but simple objects.

Tutorial Links

The official Avro documentation page (*http://bit.ly/1CVIl30*) is a great place to get started and provides "getting started" guides for both Java and Python. If you're more interested in diving straight into integrating Avro with MapReduce, you can't go wrong with the avro-mr-sample project (*http://bit.ly/1FyNXNJ*) on GitHub.

Example Code

Avro supports two general models:

- A traditional serialization model where a developer authors a schema, runs a compiler to create models based on that schema, and then uses those models in their application
- A runtime model where Avro builds records based on a schema file provided at runtime

In our example, we'll use the runtime model because this is one of the most interesting differentiators for Avro.

We start out by defining a schema in a file that we'll call *review.avsc*:

```
{"namespace": "example.elephant",
 "type": "record",
 "name": "Review",
 "fields": [
     {"name": "reviewer", "type": "string"},
     {"name": "movieTitle",  "type": "string"},
     {"name": "rating", "type": "int"}
 ]
}
```

Now we can create an object based on this schema and write it out to disk:

```
//Bind the schema
Schema schema = new Parser().parse(new File("review.avsc"));

//Build a record
GenericRecord review = new GenericData.Record(schema);
review.put("reviewer", "Kevin");
review.put("movieTitle", "Dune");
review.put("rating", 10);

// Serialize our review to disk
File file = new File("review.avro");
DatumWriter<GenericRecord> datumWriter =
    new GenericDatumWriter<GenericRecord>(schema);
DataFileWriter<GenericRecord> dataFileWriter =
    new DataFileWriter<GenericRecord>(datumWriter);
dataFileWriter.create(schema, file);
dataFileWriter.append(user1);
dataFileWriter.append(user2);
dataFileWriter.close();
```

We can also deserialize that file we just created to populate a review object:

```
//Bind the schema
Schema schema = new Parser().parse(new File("review.avsc"));

File file = new File("review.avro");
DatumReader<GenericRecord> datumReader =
    new GenericDatumReader<GenericRecord>(schema);
DataFileReader<GenericRecord> dataFileReader =
    new DataFileReader<GenericRecord>(file, datumReader);
GenericRecord review = null;

while (dataFileReader.hasNext()) {
// Reuse user object by passing it to next(). This saves us from
// allocating and garbage collecting many objects for files with
// many items.
    review = dataFileReader.next(review);
}
```

JSON

License	http://www.json.org/license.html
Activity	Medium
Purpose	Data description and transfer
Official Page	http://www.json.org
Hadoop Integration	No Integration

As JSON is not part of Hadoop, you may wonder why it's included here. Increasingly, JSON is becoming common in Hadoop because it implements a key-value view of the world. JSON is an acronym for Java Script Object Notation, and is a convenient way to describe, serialize, and transfer data. It's easy to learn and understand, and is easily parsable, self-describing, and hierarchical. In addition, JSON syntax is fairly simple. Data is represented by name-value pairs and is comma separated. Objects are enclosed by curly brackets, and arrays are enclosed by square brackets.

JSON is often compared to XML because both are used in data description and data transfer. While you'll find XML is perhaps a richer and more extensible method of serializing and describing data, you may also find that it is more difficult to read and parse. The Hadoop community seems to favor JSON rather than XML. That said, many of the configuration files in the Hadoop infrastructure are written in XML, so a basic knowledge of XML is still required to maintain a Hadoop cluster.

Tutorial Links

JSON has become one of the most widely adopted standards for sharing data. As a result, there's a wealth of information available on the Internet, including this w3schools article (*http://bit.ly/1z5nnGr*).

Example Code

Our movie review data can easily be expressed in JSON.

For example, here's the original data:

```
Kevin,Dune,10
Marshall,Dune,1
Kevin,Casablanca,5
Bob,Blazing Saddles,9
```

And here's the JSON-formatted data (the reviews are described as a collection called movieReviews, which consists of an array of a collection of name-value pairs—one for the name of the reviewer, one for the name of the move, and one for the rating):

```
{
"movieReviews": [
    { "reviewer":"Kevin", "movie":"Dune", "rating","10" },
    { "reviewer":"Marshall", "movie":"Dune", "rating","1" },
    { "reviewer":"Kevin", "movie":"Casablanca", "rating","5" },
    { "reviewer":"Bob", "movie":"Blazing Saddles", "rating","9" }
]
}
```

Protocol Buffers (protobuf)

License	BSD Simplified
Activity	Medium
Purpose	Data Serialization
Official Page	*https://developers.google.com/protocol-buffers*
Hadoop Integration	API Compatible

One common theme you'll see expressed throughout this book is the trade-off between flexibility and performance. Sometimes you want to easily share data with other folks and you're willing to take a hit in performance to make sure that data is easy to consume. There will be other occasions where you need to maximize your performance and find that you're willing to trade away flexibility in order to get it—on those occasions, you're going to want to take a look at Protocol Buffers.

The primary reason for this trade-off is that Protocol Buffers is *compile-time assembled.* This means you need to define the precise structure for your data when you build your application, a stark contrast to Avro's *runtime assembly,* which allows you to define the structure of your data while the application is running, or JSON's even more flexible, schema-less design. The upside of compile-time assembly is the code that actually serializes and deserializes your data is likely to be more optimized, and you do not need to pay the cost of building that code while your application is running.

Protocol Buffers is intended to be fast, simple, and small. As a result, it has less support for programming languages and complex data types than other serialization frameworks such as Thrift.

Tutorial Links

Google provides excellent tutorials for a variety of languages in the official project documentation (*http://bit.ly/1yjEVlk*).

Example Code

Unlike Avro (described on page 45), which supports runtime schema binding, protobuf must be integrated into your development and build process. You begin by defining a model in a *.proto* file. For example:

```
message Review {
  required string reviewer = 1;
  required string movieTitle = 2;
  required int32 rating = 3;
}
```

You then run a protobuf compiler for your specific development language (e.g., Java) to generate code based on your model definition.

The mechanism for working with the objects generated by the protobuf compiler changes slightly from language to language. In Java, we use a builder to create a new, writeable object:

```
Review.Builder reviewBuilder = Review.newBuilder();
reviewBuilder.setReviewer("Kevin");
reviewBuilder.setMovieTitle("Dune");
reviewBuilder.setRating(10);

Review review = reviewBuilder.build();
```

This review object can then be written to any sort of output stream:

```
FileOutputStream output = new FileOutputStream("review.dat");
review.writeTo(output);
```

Repopulating objects from previously serialized data is done in a similar fashion:

```
FileInputStream input = new FileInputStream("review.dat");
review.parseFrom(input);
```

Parquet

License	Apache License, Version 2.0
Activity	Medium
Purpose	File Format
Official Page	*http://parquet.io*
Hadoop Integration	API Compatible

One of the most compelling ideas behind an open ecosystem of tools, such as Hadoop, is the ability to choose the right tool for each specific job. For example, you have a choice between tools like distcp (described on page 95) or Flume (described on page 93) for moving your data into your cluster; Java MapReduce or Pig for building big data processing jobs; Puppet (described on page 61) or Chef (described on page 63) for managing your cluster; and so on. This choice differs from many traditional platforms that offer a single tool for each job and provides flexibility at the cost of complexity.

Parquet is one choice among many for managing the way your data is stored. It is a columnar data storage format, which means it performs very well with data that is structured and has a fair amount of repetition. On the other hand, the Parquet format is fairly complex and does not perform as well in cases where you want to retrieve entire records of data at a time.

Tutorial Links

The GitHub page for the Parquet format (*http://bit.ly/1zWkxHi*) project is a great place to start if you're interested in learning a bit more about how the technology works. If, on the other hand, you'd like to dive straight into examples, move over to the GitHub page for the parquet m/r project (*http://bit.ly/1KJbOx8*).

Example Code

The Parquet file format is supported by many of the standard Hadoop tools, including Hive (described on page 34) and Pig (described on page 76). Using the Parquet data format is typically as easy as adding a couple lines to your CREATE TABLE command or changing a few words in your Pig script.

For example, to change our Hive example to use Parquet instead of the delimited textfile format, we simply refer to Parquet when we create the table:

```
CREATE EXTERNAL TABLE movie_reviews
    ( reviewer STRING, title STRING, rating INT)
ROW FORMAT SERDE 'parquet.hive.serde.ParquetHiveSerDe'
STORED
    INPUTFORMAT "parquet.hive.DeprecatedParquetInputFormat"
    OUTPUTFORMAT "parquet.hive.DeprecatedParquetOutputFormat"
    LOCATION '/data/reviews';
```

We can similarly modify our Pig example to load a review file that is stored in the Parquet format instead of CSV:

```
reviews = load 'reviews.pqt' using parquet.pig.ParquetLoader
    as (reviewer:chararray, title:chararray, rating:int);
```

## CHAPTER 4

Management and Monitoring

Building and keeping tabs on a big data architecture can be a daunting task. You've got a diverse set of software spread out across many machines that might have dramatically different configurations. How can you tell if part of your system is failing, and how do you bring that component back up after you've fixed the problem? How can the different parts of your system communicate with on another so they can do big jobs with many moving parts?

Fortunately, the big data ecosystem provides a variety of tools to ease the burden of managing and monitoring your architecture. We're going to address three primary categories of these tools:

Node configuration management
> These are tools like Puppet or Chef that can help you manage the configuration of your systems. They do things like change operating system parameters and install software.

Resource tracking
> While many individual components in your architecture may come with tools to monitor the performance of that specific component, sometimes you need a single dashboard or insight into something that isn't tied to a specific tool.

Coordination
> Many tasks take advantage of a handful of different components of your big data system. Tools like ZooKeeper can help you synchronize all those moving parts to accomplish a single goal.

Ambari

 Apache Ambari
http://incubator.apache.org/ambari

License	Apache License, Version 2.0
Activity	High
Purpose	Provisioning, monitoring, and management of a Hadoop cluster
Official Page	*http://ambari.apache.org*
Hadoop Integration	Fully Integrated

If you've ever tried to install Hadoop from the Apache download, you'll know that Hadoop is still a bear to install and manage. Recently, Pivotal and Hortonworks, two of the major vendors, agreed to work jointly on Ambari in an attempt to produce a production-ready, easy-to-use, web-based GUI tool based on a RESTful API.

The Ambari documentation at the official page says that it can:

- Provision and monitor a Hadoop cluster
- Provide a step-by-step wizard for installing Hadoop services across any number of hosts
- Provide central management for starting, stopping, and reconfiguring Hadoop services across the entire cluster
- Provide a dashboard for monitoring health and status of the Hadoop cluster
- Leverage Ganglia (described on page 71) for metrics collection
- Leverage Nagios (described on page 60) for system alerting

While installing Hadoop with traditional methods might be a multi-day ordeal, Ambari can accomplish this in a few hours with relative ease. Ambari graduated from Incubator status to Top Level Project late in 2013 and should now be ready for production use.

Tutorial Links

There is a silent video (*http://youtu.be/xeT3A1nha6g*) that takes you through a cluster build with Ambari.

Here's a great slideshow tutorial (*http://slidesha.re/16SvC1L*).

Example Code

Ambari is a GUI-based tool, so there's no way we can present a code example.

HCatalog

HCatalog
Table Management

License	Apache License, Version 2.0
Activity	High
Purpose	Data abstraction layer
Official Page	*http://hive.apache.org/javadocs/hcat-r0.5.0/index.html*
Hadoop Integration	Fully Integrated

Suppose you have a set of files that you access with MapReduce, Hive, and Pig. Wouldn't it be useful if you had a way of accessing them so that you didn't have to know details of file format and location? You do. HCatalog provides an abstraction layer on many file types in HDFS allowing users of Pig, Hive, and MapReduce to concentrate on reading and writing their data without detailed consideration of what format it is using. This abstraction layer makes the data look very much like relational data (i.e., arranged in tables with rows and columns and a very SQL-like feel). HCatalog is closely associated with Hive because it uses and derives from the Hive metastore, the place that Hive stores its metadata about its tables.

HCatalog has the notion of partitions. A partition is a subset of rows of a table that have some common characteristic. Often, tables are partitioned by a date field. This makes it easy to query and also easy to manage, dropping partitions when they are no longer needed.

If you decide to use HCatalog, you'll access your data via the HCatalog methods rather than those native to Pig or MapReduce. For example, in Pig, you commonly use PigStorage or TextLoader to read data, whereas when using HCatalog, you would use HCatLoader and HCatStorer.

Tutorial Links

HCatalog is one of the more sparsely documented major projects in the Hadoop ecosystem, but this tutorial (*http://youtu.be/ _dVlNu4lqpE*) from HortonWorks is well done.

Example Code

In Pig without HCatalog, you might load a file using something like:

```
reviews = load 'reviews.csv' using PigStorage(',')
    as (reviewer:chararray, title:chararray,rating:int);
```

Using HCatalog, you might first create a table within Hive

```
CREATE TABLE movie_reviews
    ( reviewer STRING, title STRING, rating INT)
ROW FORMAT DELIMITED
FIELDS TERMINATED BY '|'
STORED AS TEXTFILE
```

and then use it in your Pig statement:

```
reviews = load 'movie_reviews'
USING org.apache.hcatalog.pig.HCatLoader(); -
```

Nagios

Nagios®

License	GNU General Public License
Activity	High
Purpose	IT infrastructure monitoring
Official Page	*http://www.nagios.org*
Hadoop Integration	No Integration

As anyone who has ever been responsible for a networked computer system knows, keeping track of what's happening in such a network is of critical importance. You need to know when things go wrong by being alerted rather than manually polling. You would like to have automated restart of failed components. You would like a tool that presents a graphical interface so you can quickly see what's happening in the environment. Nagios is such a tool. Like many products in the open source world, there is a version that you can freely download, and expanded versions that are licensed at a cost.

The open source core product has many useful features. It provides monitoring of servers, switches, OS, and application through a web-based interface. More important, it provides quick detection of outages and problems and can alert your operations staff via email or text message. There are provisions for automatic restart.

Importantly, Nagios can be embedded into other systems, including Ambari (described on page 56).

Tutorial Links

The Nagios main site has a live demo system (*http://bit.ly/1Chq6yn*).

There are a score of others, including this page on Debian Help (*http://bit.ly/1zLS1JC*) and this one on TuxRadar (*http://bit.ly/1CgXTuc*).

Puppet

License	Apache License, Version 2.0
Activity	High
Purpose	Node Management
Official Page	*https://puppetlabs.com*
Hadoop Integration	API Compatible

Puppet is a popular system for managing the configuration of large numbers of machines. It uses a "declarative" syntax, which means you describe the configuration of your machines and Puppet takes care of figuring out the steps necessary to achieve that configuration. For example, you will describe a configuration that has certain programs installed and Puppet will take care of figuring out how to determine if those programs are installed and how to install them if they are not yet installed.

Puppet configurations are written in terms of resources, manifests, and modules. A resource is the most basic unit of configuration and represents the state of a specific thing. For example, a resource might state that a specific file should exist and that everyone should be able to view its contents, but only the system administrator should be able to alter its contents.

The next level of configuration is a manifest. A manifest is a group of related resources. For example, a manifest may say that installing your application requires both a specific version of a RedHat Package Manager (RPM) to be installed, and that a configuration directory be created.

A module is a logical group of related, but separate, manifests. For example, a module for our application might contain one manifest that installs our application, another manifest that configures our application to work with an HBase instance (described on page 19), and a third module that configures our application to send logs to a specific location.

Tutorial Links

Puppet Labs provides a variety of resources (*http://bit.ly/17gLBYA*) for those getting started.

Example Code

Puppet manifests are written in Ruby and follow typical Ruby syntax rules.

Our example manifest to install our application and ensure the configuration directory exists would look like this:

```
# 'test_application.pp'
class test_application {
    package { 'test_application':
        ensure => installed
    }

    file { 'test_application_conf':
        path => '/etc/test_application/conf',
        ensure => directory,
        require => Package['test_application']
    }
}
```

Chef

License	Apache License, Version 2.0
Activity	High
Purpose	Node Management
Official Page	*https://www.getchef.com*
Hadoop Integration	API Compatible

Chef is designed to ease the burden of managing the configuration of your infrastructure. It follows an "imperative" syntax that is familiar to many software developers, allowing them to write software configuration the same we they write software code.

Chef configurations are written as resources, recipes, and cookbooks. A resource is the most basic unit of configuration and describes how to configure a specific thing. For example, a resource might tell Chef to create a specific directory and to make sure that everyone is able to view its contents, but that the contents can only be altered by the system administrator.

The next level of configuration is a recipe. A recipe is a group of related resources. For example, a recipe may say that installing your application takes two steps: first you must install a specific package, and then you must create a configuration directory.

A cookbook is a logical group of related, but separate, recipes. For example, a module for our application might contain one recipe that installs our application, another recipe that configures our application to work with an HBase instance (described on page 19), and a third recipe that configures our application to work with an Accumulo instance (described on page 22). All three of these manifests relate to installing and configuring our application, but we need to be be able to control which of these manifests is actually run without being required to run them all.

Tutorial

Opscode provides a variety of resources for getting started on its wiki page (*https://wiki.opscode.com*).

Example Code

Chef recipes are written in Ruby and follow typical Ruby syntax rules.

Our example manifest to install our application and ensure the configuration directory exists would look like this:

```
# 'default.rb'
package "test_application" do
    action :install
end

directory "/etc/test_application/conf" do
    action :create
end
```

ZooKeeper

License	Apache License, Version 2.0
Activity	Medium
Purpose	Coordination
Official Page	*https://zookeeper.apache.org*
Hadoop Integration	API Compatible

Hadoop and HDFS are effective tools for distributing work across many machines, but sometimes you need to quickly share little bits of information between a number of simultaneously running processes. ZooKeeper is built for exactly this sort of need: it's an effective mechanism for storing and sharing small amounts of state and configuration data across many machines.

For example, let's say you have a job that takes information from a large number of small files, transforms that data, and puts the information into a database.

You could store the information in a file on a fileshare or in HDFS, but accessing that information from many machines can be very slow and attempting to update the information can be difficult due to synchronization issues.

A slightly better approach would be to move the connection information into a MapReduce job configuration file. Even then, you would need to update a file for every analytic every time the database moves. Also, there would be no straightforward way to update the connection information if the database needs to be moved while you have an analytic running.

Better still, storing the connection information in ZooKeeper allows your analytics to quickly access the information while also providing a simple mechanism for updates.

ZooKeeper is not intended to fill the space of HBase (described on page 19) or any other big data key-value store. In fact, there are protections built into ZooKeeper to ensure that folks do not attempt to use it as a large data store. ZooKeeper is, however, just right when all you want to do is share a little bit of information across your environment.

Tutorial Links

The official getting started guide (*http://bit.ly/1DFmPNU*) is a great place to get your feet wet with ZooKeeper.

Example Code

In this example, we're going to start by opening the ZooKeeper command-line interface:

```
$ zookeeper-client
```

Now we'll create a key-value pair. In this case, the key is /movie_reviews/database and the value is the IP address of a database we'll use for our movie reviews:

```
[zk: localhost:3000(CONNECTED) 0] create /movie_reviews ''
Created /movie_reviews

[zk: localhost:3000(CONNECTED) 1] create /movie_reviews/database
'10.2.1.1'
Created /movie_reviews/database
```

Now we'll retrieve the value for our key. Notice that we get back two important pieces of data—the actual value of *10.2.1.1* and the version of the value:

```
[zk: localhost:3000(CONNECTED) 2] get /movie_reviews/database
'10.2.1.1'
<metadata>
dataVersion = 0
<metadata>
```

Imagine the original server hosting our database has crashed and we need to point all the different processes that use that database to our failover. We'll update the value associated with our key to point to the IP address of our failover:

```
[zk: localhost:3000(CONNECTED) 0] set /movie_reviews/database
'10.2.1.2'
<metadata>
dataVersion = 1
<metadata>
```

Now let's get the key one last time. Notice that we retrieve the new IP address and the version has incremented to indicate that the value has changed:

```
[zk: localhost:3000(CONNECTED) 1] get /movie_reviews/database
'10.2.1.2'
<metadata>
dataVersion = 1
<metadata>
```

Oozie

License	Apache License, Version 2.0
Activity	High
Purpose	A workflow scheduler to manage complex multipart Hadoop jobs
Official Page	*https://oozie.apache.org*
Hadoop Integration	Fully Integrated

You may be able to complete some of your data analytic tasks with a single MapReduce, Pig, or Hive job that reads its data from the Hadoop Distributed File System (HDFS, described on page 3), computes its output and stores it in HDFS, but some tasks will be more complicated. For example, you may have a job that requires that two or three other jobs finish, and each of these require that data is loaded into HDFS from some external source. And you may want to run this job on a periodic basis. Of course, you could orchestrate this manually or by some clever scripting, but there is an easier way.

That way is Oozie, Hadoop's workflow scheduler. It's a bit complicated at first, but has some useful power to start, stop, suspend, and restart jobs, and control the workflow so that no task within the complete job runs before the tasks and objects it requires are ready. Oozie puts its actions (jobs and tasks) in a directed acyclic graph (DAG) that describe what actions depend upon previous actions completing successfully. This is defined in a large XML file (actually hPDL, Hadoop Process Definition Language). The file is too large to display here for any nontrivial example, but the tutorials and Oozie site have examples.

What is a DAG? A graph is a collection of nodes and arcs. Nodes represent states or objects. Arcs connect the nodes. If an arc has an arrow at either end, then that arc is directed and the direction of the arrow indicates the direction. In Oozie, the nodes are the actions, such as to run a job, fork, fail, or end. The arcs show which actions flow into others. It's directed to show the ordering of the actions and decision or controls—that is, what nodes must run jobs or whether events precede or follow (e.g., a file object must be present before a Pig script is run). Acyclic means that in traversing the graph, once you leave a node, you cannot get back there. That would be a cycle. An implication of this is that Oozie cannot be used to iterate through a set of nodes until a condition is met (i.e., there are no while loops). There is more information about graphs in "Giraph" on page 39.

Figure 4-1 is a graphic example of an Oozie flow in which a Hive job requires the output of both a Pig job and a MapReduce job, both of which require external files to be present.

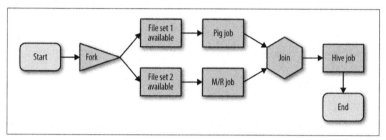

Figure 4-1. Graph representation of Oozie job flow

The Oozie installation comes with a GUI console for job monitoring, but it requires the use of Ext JS, a JavaScript framework for building desktop apps that comes with both open source and commercial versions.

Recently there has been some use of Hue as a more general Hadoop monitoring tool. Hue is open source, distributed under the Apache License, Version 2.0 and is primarily associated with the Cloudera Hadoop Distribution.

Tutorial Links

There are a handful of interesting Oozie presentations, including this one by IBM's big data team (*http://youtu.be/ypn7dGkD3mA*) and this academic presentation (*http://youtu.be/GGRhSEE45tk*).

Example Code

The actual example files are too large to easily fit here. For more information, refer to the official user resources page (*http://bit.ly/1EYrsnK*), which contains cookbooks for a variety of languages.

Ganglia

License	BSD
Activity	Medium
Purpose	Monitoring
Official Page	*http://ganglia.sourceforge.net*
Hadoop Integration	API Compatible

Ganglia is a distributed monitoring system specifically designed to work with clusters and grids consisting of many machines. It allows you to quickly visualize how your systems are being used and can be a useful tool for keeping track of the general welfare of your cluster. Ganglia is best used to understand how your system is behaving at a very broad but very shallow level. Folks who are looking to debug or optimize specific analytics would be better served to look at other tools that are geared toward providing much deeper information at a much narrower scope, such as White Elephant.

By default, Ganglia is capable of providing information about much of the inner workings of your system right out of the box. This includes a number of data points describing such things as how much of your total computing capability is being used, how much data is moving through your network, and how your persistent storage is being utilized. Users with additional needs can also extend Ganglia to capture and display more information, such as application-specific metrics, through the use of plug-ins. Hadoop is packaged with a set of plug-ins for reporting information about HDFS and MapReduce to Ganglia (see the Ganglia Metrics (*http://bit.ly/1ITRL1r*) project for more information).

Ganglia is being used in the Ambari project (described on page 56).

Tutorial Links

Ganglia has a widely distributed support network (*http://bit.ly/ 1CgY34H*) spanning mailing lists, GitHub defect tracking, wiki pages, and more. An excellent starting off point for folks looking to get their first Ganglia installation working is the Ganglia wiki page (*http://bit.ly/1vkfVXp*).

Example Code

Configuring a Ganglia instance is beyond the scope of this book, as is even the most basic of distributed system monitoring and diagnostic processes. Interested readers are encouraged to look at the Ganglia instance monitoring the Wikimedia (Wikipedia) cluster (*http://bit.ly/1FyOQpx*) to see Ganglia in action.

## CHAPTER 5

Analytic Helpers

Now that you've ingested data into your Hadoop cluster, what's next? Usually you'll want to start by simply cleansing or transforming your data. This could be as simple or reformatting fields and removing corrupt records or it could involve all manner of complex aggregation, enrichment, and summarization. Once you've cleaned up your data, you may be satisfied to simply push it into a more traditional data store, such as a relational database, and consider your big data work to be done. On the other hand, you may want to continue to work with your data, running specialized machine-learning algorithms to categorize your data or perhaps performing some sort of geospatial analysis.

In this chapter, we're going to talk about two types of tools:

MapReduce interfaces
> General-purpose tools that make it easier to process your data

Analytic libraries
> Focused-purpose libraries that include functionality to make it easier to analyze your data

MapReduce Interfaces

In the early days of Hadoop, the only way to process the data in your system was to work with MapReduce in Java, but this approach presented a couple of major problems:

- Your analytic writers need to not only understand your business and your data, but they also need to understand Java code

- Pushing a Java archive to Hadoop is more time-consuming than simply authoring a query

For example, the process of developing and testing a simple analytic written directly in MapReduce might look something like the following for a developer:

1. Write about a hundred lines of Java MapReduce.

2. Compile the code into a JAR file (Java archive).

3. Copy the JAR file to cluster.

4. Run the analytic.

5. Find a bug, go back and write some more code.

As you can imagine, this process can be time-consuming, and tinkering with the code can disrupt thinking about the business problem. Fortunately, a robust ecosystem of tools to work with Hadoop and MapReduce have emerged to simplify this process and allow your analysts to spend more time thinking about the business problem at hand.

As you'll see, these tools generally do a few things:

- Provide a simpler, more familiar interface to MapReduce

- Generate immediate feedback by allowing users to build queries interactively

- Simplify complex operations

Analytic Libraries

While there is much analysis that can be done in MapReduce or Pig, there are some machine-learning algorithms that are distributed as part of Apache Mahout project. Some examples of the kinds of problems suited for Mahout are classification, recommendation, and clustering.

You point machine-learning algorithms at a dataset, and they "learn" something from the data. They fall into two classes: supervised and unsupervised. In supervised learning, the data typically has a set of observations and an outcome value. For example, clinical data about patients would be the observations, and an outcome value might be the presence of a disease. A supervised-learning algorithm, given a new patient's clinical data, would try to predict the presence of a disease. Unsupervised algorithms do not use a given outcome, and instead attempt to find some hidden pattern in the data. For example, we could take a set of observations of clinical data from patients and try to see if they tend to cluster, so that points inside a cluster would be "close" to one another and the cluster centers would be far from one another. The interpretation of the cluster is not given by the algorithm and is left for the data analyst to discover. You can find the list of supported algorithms on the Mahout home page (*http://bit.ly/1vkgb8Q*).

Recommendation algorithms determine the following: based on other people's ratings, and the similarity of them to you, what would you be likely to rate highly?

Classification algorithms, given a set of observations on an individual, predict some unknown outcome. If the outcome is a binary variable, logistic regression can be used to predict the probability of that outcome. For example, given the set of lab results of a patient, predict the probability that the patient has a given disease. If the outcome is a numeric variable, linear regression can be used to predict the value of that outcome. For example, given this month's economic conditions, predict the unemployment rate for next month.

Clustering algorithms don't really answer a question. You frequently use them in the first stage of your analysis to get a feel for the data.

Data analytics is a deep topic—too deep to discuss in any detail here. O'Reilly has an excellent series of books (*http://oreil.ly/1ITSeka*) on the topic of data analytics.

Most of the analytics just discussed deal with numerical or categorical data. Increasingly important in the Hadoop world are text analytics and geospatial analytics.

Pig

License	Apache License, Version 2.0
Activity	High
Purpose	High-level data flow language for processing data
Official Page	*http://pig.apache.org*
Hadoop Integration	Fully Integrated

If MapReduce code in Java is the "assembly language" of Hadoop, then Pig is analogous to Python or another high-level language. Why would you want to use Pig rather than MapReduce? Writing in Pig may not be as performant as writing mappers and reducers in Java, but it speeds up your coding and makes it much more maintainable. Pig calls itself a data flow language in which datasets are read in and transformed to other datasets using a combination of procedural thinking as well as some SQL-like constructs.

Pig is so called because "pigs eat everything," meaning that Pig can accommodate many different forms of input, but is frequently used for transforming text datasets. In many ways, Pig is an admirable extract, transform, and load (ETL) tool. Pig is translated or compiled into MapReduce code and it is reasonably well optimized so that a series of Pig statements do not generate mappers and reducers for each statement and then run them sequentially.

There is a library of shared Pig routines available in the Piggy Bank (*http://bit.ly/1EYrPyH*).

Tutorial Links

There's a fairly complete guide (*http://bit.ly/199tCnF*) to get you through the process of installing Pig and writing your first couple scripts. "Working with Pig" (*http://youtu.be/tFsHO12eOgc*) is a great overview of the Pig technology.

Example Code

The movie review problem can be expressed quickly in Pig with only five lines of code:

```
-- Read in all the movie review and find the average rating
   for the film Dune
-- the file reviews.csv has lines of form:
   name, film_title, rating
   reviews = load 'reviews.csv' using PigStorage(',')
     as (reviewer:chararray, title:chararray,rating:int);

-- Only consider reviews of Dune
   duneonly = filter reviews by title == 'Dune';

-- we want to use the Pig builtin AVG function but
-- AVG works on bags, not lists, this creates bags
   dunebag = group duneonly by title;

-- now generate the average and then dump it
   dunescore = foreach dunebag generate AVG(dune.rating);
   dump dunescore;
```

Hadoop Streaming

License	Apache License, Version 2.0
Activity	Medium
Purpose	Write MapReduce code without Java
Official Page	*http://hadoop.apache.org/docs/r1.2.1/streaming.html*
Hadoop Integration	Fully Integrated

You have some data, you have an idea of what you want to do with it, you understand the concepts of MapReduce, but you don't have solid Java or MapReduce expertise, and the problem does not really fit into any of the other major tools that Hadoop has to offer. Your solution may be Hadoop Streaming, which allows you to write code in any Linux program that reads from stdin and writes to stdout.

You still need to write mappers and reducers, but in the language of your choice. Your mapper will likely read lines from a text file and produce a key-value pair separated by a tab character. The shuffle phase of the process will be handled by the MapReduce infrastructure, and your reducer will read from standard input (stdin), do its processing, and write its output to standard output (stdout).

The reference in the following "Tutorial Links" section shows a WordCount application in Hadoop Streaming using Python.

Is Streaming going to be as performant as native Java code? Almost certainly not, but if your organization has Ruby or Python or similar skills, you will definitely yield better results than sending your developers off to learn Java before doing any MapReduce projects.

Tutorial Links

There's an excellent overview of the technology as well as a tutorial available on this web page (*http://bit.ly/1DhVReH*).

Example Code

We'll use streaming to compute the average ranking for *Dune*. Let's start with our small dataset:

```
Kevin,Dune,10
Marshall,Dune,1
Kevin,Casablanca,5
Bob,Blazing Saddles,9
```

The mapper function could be:

```
#! /usr/bin/python

import sys

for line in sys.stdin:
    line = line.strip()
    keys = line.split(',')
    print( "%s\t%s" % (keys[1], keys[2]) )
```

The reducer function could be:

```
#!/usr/bin/python
import sys

count = 0
rating_sum = 0
for input_line in sys.stdin:
    input_line = input_line.strip()
    title, rating = input_line.split("\t", 1)
    rating = float(rating)
    if title == 'Dune':
        count += 1
        rating_sum += rating
dune_avg = rating_sum/count
print("%s\t%f" % ('Dune',dune_avg))
```

And the job would be run as:

```
hadoop jar contrib/streaming/hadoop-*streaming*.jar \
-file /home/hduser/mapper.py  \
-mapper /home/hduser/movie-mapper.py \
-file /home/hduser/reducer.py \
-reducer /home/hduser/movie-reducer.py \
-input /user/hduser/movie-reviews-in/* \
-output /user/hduser/movie-reviews-out
```

producing the result:

```
Dune    5.500000
```

Mahout

License	Apache License, Version 2.0
Activity	High
Purpose	Machine learning and data analytics
Official Page	*http://mahout.apache.org*
Hadoop Integration	API Compatible

You have a bunch of data in your Hadoop cluster. What are you going to do with it? You might want to do some analytics, or data science, or machine learning. Much of this can be done in some of the tools that come with the standard Apache distribution, such as Pig, MapReduce, or Hive. But more sophisticated uses will involve algorithms that you will not want to code yourself. So you turn to Mahout. What is Mahout? Mahout is a collection of scalable machine-learning algorithms that run on Hadoop. Why is it called Mahout? Mahout is the Hindi word for an elephant handler, as you can see from the logo. The list of algorithms is constantly growing, but as of March 2014, it includes the ones listed in Table 5-1.

Table 5-1. Mahout MapReduce algorithms

Mahout algorithm	Brief description
k-means/fuzzy *k*-means clustering	Clustering is dividing a set of observation into groups where elements in the group are similar and the groups are distinct
Latent Dirichlet allocation	LDA is a modelling technique often used for classifying documents predicated on the use of specific topic terms in the document

Mahout algorithm	Brief description
Singular value decomposition	SVD is difficult to explain succinctly without a lot of linear algebra and eigenvalue background
Logistic-regression-based classifier	Logistic regression is used to predict variables that have a zero-one value, such as presence or absense of a disease, or membership in a group
Complementary naive Bayes classifier	Another classification scheme making use of Bayes' theorem (which you may remember from Statistics 101)
Random forest decision tree-based classifier	Yet another classifier based on decision trees
Collaborative filtering	Used in recommendation systems (if you like X, may we suggest Y)

A fuller discussion of all these is well beyond the scope of this book. There are many good introductions to machine learning available. Google is your friend here.

In April 2014, the Mahout community announced that it was moving away from MapReduce to a domain-specific language (DSL) based on Scala to a Spark implementation (described on page 10). Current MapReduce algorithms would continue to be supported, but additions to the code base could not be MapReduce based. In fact, in the latest release, the Mahout community had dropped support for some infrequently used routines.

Tutorial Links

The Mahout folks have an entire page of curated links to books, tutorials, and talks (*http://bit.ly/1zLSJqu*).

Example Code

The process of using Mahout to produce a recommendation system is too complex to present here. Mahout includes an example of a movie ratings recommendation system (*http://bit.ly/1zLSKKM*). The data is available via GroupLens Research (*http://bit.ly/1vEPilR*).

MLLib

License	Apache License, Version 2.0
Activity	High
Purpose	Machine-learning tools for Spark
Official Page	*https://spark.apache.org/mllib*
Hadoop Integration	Fully Integrated

If you've decided to invest in Spark but need some machine-learning tools, then MLLib provides you with a basic set. Similar in functionality to Mahout (described on page 81), MLLib has an ever-growing list of modules that perform many tasks useful to data scientists and big data analytics teams. As of Version 1.2, the list includes (but is not limited to) those in Table 5-2. New algorithms are frequently added.

Table 5-2. MLLib algorithms

MLLib algorithm	Brief description
Linear SVM and logistic regression	Prediction using continuous and binary variables
Classification and regression tree	Methods to classify data based on binary decisions
k-means clustering	Clustering is dividing a set of observation into groups where elements in the group are similar and the groups are distinct
Recommendation via alternating least squares	Used in recommendation systems (if you like X, you might like Y)
Multinomial naive Bayes	Classification based upon Bayes' Theorem
Basic statistics	Summary statistics, random data generation, correlations

MLLib algorithm	Brief description
Feature extraction and transformation	A number of routines often used in text analytics
Dimensionality reduction	Reducing the number of variables in an analytic problem, often used when they are highly correlated

Again, as MLLib lives on Spark, you would be wise to know Scala, Python, or Java to do anything sophisticated with it.

You may wonder whether to choose MLLib or Mahout. In the short run, Mahout is more mature and has a larger set of routines, but the current version of Mahout uses MapReduce and is slower in general (though likely more stable). If the algorithms you need only exist today on Mahout, that solves your problem. Mahout currently has a much larger user community, so if you're looking for online help with problems, you're more likely to find it for Mahout. On the other hand, Mahout v2 will move to Spark and Scala, so in the long run, MLLib may well replace Mahout or they may merge efforts.

Tutorial Links

"MLLib: Scalable Machine Learning on Spark" (*http://stanford.io/ 1E9CGlF*) is a thorough but rather technical tutorial that you may find useful.

Example Code

The AMPlab at Berkeley has some example code (*http://bit.ly/ 1CgYmMV*) to do personalized movie recommendations based on collaborative filtering.

Hadoop Image Processing Interface (HIPI)

License	BSD Simplified
Activity	Moderate
Purpose	Image Processing
Official Page	*http://hipi.cs.virginia.edu/index.html*
Hadoop Integration	API Compatible

Image processing is a vastly overloaded term. It can mean something as simple as "cleaning up" your image by putting it into focus and making the boundaries more distinct. It can also mean determining what is in your image, or scene analysis. For example, does the image of a lung X-ray show a tumor? Does the image of cells collected in a Pap smear indicate potential cervical cancer? Or it can mean deciding whether a fingerprint image matches a particular image or is similar to one in a set of images.

HIPI is an image-processing package under development at the University of Virginia. While the documentation is sketchy, the main use is the examination of a collection of images and determining their similarity or dissimilarity. This package seems to assume a knowledge of image processing and specific technologies such as the exchangeable image file format (EXIF). As this is a university project, its future is unknown, but there seems to be a resurgence of activity expected in 2015, including Spark integration.

Tutorial Links

HIPI is still a fairly new technology; the best source of information at the moment is this thesis paper (*http://bit.ly/1FyPjYS*).

Example Code

A number of examples of HIPI usage can be found on the project's official examples page (*http://bit.ly/1zWlFe4*).

SpatialHadoop

License	Unknown
Activity	High
Purpose	Spatial Analytics
Official Page	*http://spatialhadoop.cs.umn.edu*
Hadoop Integration	API Compatible

If you've been doing much work with spatial data, it's likely you're familiar with PostGIS, the open source spatial extension to the open source PostgreSQL database. But what if you want to work in a massively Hadoop environment rather than PostgreSQL? The University of Minnesota's computer science department has developed SpatialHadoop, which is an open source extension to MapReduce designed to process huge datasets of spatial data in Hadoop. To use SpatialHadoop, you first load data into HDFS and then build a spatial index. Once you index the data, you can execute any of the spatial operations provided in SpatialHadoop such as range query, k-nearest neighbor, and spatial join.

There are high-level calls in SHadoop that generate MapReduce jobs, so it's possible to use SHadoop without writing MapReduce code. There are clear usage examples at the website.

In addition to the MapReduce implementation, there is an extension to Pig, called Pigeon, that allows spatial queries in Pig Latin. This is available at the project page in GitHub (*http://bit.ly/1zWlJdY*). Pigeon has the stated goal of supporting as many of the PostGIS functions as possible. This is an ambitious but extremely useful goal because PostGIS has a wide following and the ST functions it supports make it fairly simple to do spatial analytics in a high-level language like Pig/Pigeon.

The code is all open source and available on GitHub (*http://bit.ly/1ITT0gY*).

Tutorial Links

The official project page has a handful of links to great tutorials (*http://bit.ly/1Md6lQQ*).

CHAPTER 6
Data Transfer

Data transfer deals with three important questions:

- How do you get data into a Hadoop cluster?
- How do you get data out of a Hadoop cluster?
- How do you move data from one Hadoop cluster to another Hadoop cluster?

In general, Hadoop is not a transactional engine, where data is loaded in small, discrete, related bits of information like it would be in an airline reservation system. Instead, data is bulk loaded from external sources such a flat files for sensors, bulk loads from sources like *http://www.data.gov* for U.S. federal government data or log files, or transfers from relational systems.

The Hadoop ecosystem contains a variety of great tools for working with your data. However, it's rare for your data to start or end in Hadoop. It's much more common to have a workflow that starts with data from external systems, such as logs from your web servers, and ends with analytics hosted on a business intelligence (BI) system.

Data transfer tools help move data between those systems. More specifically, data transfer tools provide three basic capabilities:

File transfer
> Tools like Flume (described on page 93) and DistCp (described on page 95) help move files and flat text, such as long entries, into your Hadoop cluster.

Database transfer
> Tools like Sqoop (described next) provide a simple mechanism for moving data between traditional relational databases, such as Oracle or SQL Server, and your Hadoop cluster.

Data triage
> Tools like Storm (described on page 97) can be used to quickly evaluate and categorize new data as it arrives onto your Hadoop system.

Sqoop

License	Apache License, Version 2.0
Activity	High
Purpose	Transfer data from HDFS to and from relational databases
Official Page	*http://sqoop.apache.org*
Hadoop Integration	Fully Integrated

It's likely that some of your data may originate in a relational database management system (RDBMS) that is usually accessed normally by SQL. You could also use your SQL engine to produce flat files to load into HDFS. While dumps may load large datasets more quickly, you may have reason to take data directly from an RDMBS or place the results of your Hadoop processing into an RDBMS. Sqoop (meaning SQL to Hadoop) is designed to transfer data between Hadoop clusters and relational databases. It's a top-level Apache project developed by Cloudera, now in the public domain. While Sqoop automates much of the process, some SQL knowledge is required to have this work properly. The Sqoop job is then transformed into a MapReduce job that does the work.

You'll start your import to Hadoop with a database table that is read into Hadoop as a text file or in Avro or SequenceFile format. You can also export an HDFS file into an RDBMS. In this case, the Map-Reduce job reads a set of text-delimited files in HDFS in parallel and converts them into rows in an RDBMS. There are options to filter rows and columns, alter delimiters, and more.

Tutorial Links

There's an excellent series of lectures on this topic available on YouTube. Once you've watched Apache Sqoop Tutorial Part 1 (*http:// youtu.be/8NzcZzCrOcU*), you can jump to Parts 2 (*http://youtu.be/*

pwjlk-w4VC0), 3 *(http://youtu.be/Oz52SS3XeE0)*, and 4 *(http:// youtu.be/-bZ0AuyBg3I)*.

Example Code

Our movie review dataset is in a table in a PostgreSQL database, and we want to import it into a text file in Hadoop (it is also possible to move data from Hadoop to an RDBMS, but this is not illustrated here):

```
myschema=> select * from moviereviews
reviewer  |     title      | score
----------+----------------+-------
Kevin     | Dune           |   10
Kevin     | Casablanca     |    5
Bob       | Blazing Saddles|    9
Marshall  | Dune           |    1


sqoop import --connect jdbc:postgresql://<host>/<database> \
    --table moviereviews --username JoeUser --P

<lots of lines omitted>

hadoop fs -cat moviereviews/part-m-00000
Kevin,Dune,10
Kevin,Casablanca,5
Bob, Blazing Saddles,9
Marshall,Dune,1
```

Flume

License	Apache License, Version 2.0
Activity	Medium
Purpose	Data collection and aggregation, especially for log data
Official Page	*http://flume.apache.org*
Hadoop Integration	Fully Integrated

You have identified data that lives in a feeder system that you'll need in your Hadoop cluster to do some analysis and now need to find a way to move it there. In general, you cannot use FTP or SCP, as these transport data between POSIX-compliant filesystems and HDFS is not POSIX compliant. Some Hadoop distributions, such as the MapR distribution or those that are certified to use the Isilon OneFS, can accommodate this. You could FTP the data to the native filesystem on a Hadoop node and then use HDFS commands like copyFromLocal, but this is tedious and single threaded. Flume to the rescue!

Flume is a reliable distributed system for collecting, aggregating, and moving large amounts of log data from multiple sources into HDFS. It supports complex multihop flows and fan-in and fan-out. Events are staged in a channel on each agent and delivered to the next agent in the chain, finally removed once they reach the next agent or HDFS, the ultimate sink. A Flume process has a configuration file that list the sources, sinks, and channels for the data flow. Typical use cases include loading log data into Hadoop.

Tutorial Links

Dr. Dobb's Journal published an informative article (*http://ubm.io/ 199uad3*) on Flume. Readers who enjoy a lecture should check out this interesting presentation (*http://youtu.be/POJCV28UYe4*) from 2011.

Example Code

To use Flume, you'll first build a configuration file that describes the agent: the source, the sink, and the channel. Here the source is net-cat, a program that echoes output through TCP, the sink is an HDFS file, and the channel is a memory channel:

```
# xmpl.conf

# Name the components on this agent
agent1.sources = src1
agent1.sinks = snk1
agent1.channels = chn1

# Describe/configure the source
agent1.sources.src1.type = exec
agent.sources.src1.command = tail -F /var/log/system.log
agent.sources.src1.channels = memory-channel

# Describe the sink
agent1.sinks.snk1.channel = memory-channel
agent1.sinks.snk1.type = hdfs
agent1.sinks.snk1.hdfs.path = hdfs://n1:54310/tmp/system.log/
agent1.sinks.snk1.hdfs.fileType = DataStream

# Use a channel which buffers events in memory
agent1.channels.chn1.type = memory
agent1.channels.chn1.capacity = 1000
agent1.channels.chn1.transactionCapacity = 100

# Bind the source and sink to the channel
agent1.sources.src1.channels = c1
agent1.sinks.snk1.channel = c1

# Then start the agent.  As the lines are added to the log file,
# they will be pushed to the memory channel and then to the
# HDFS file_

flume-ng agent --conf conf --conf-file xmpl.conf --name agent1 \
    -Dflume.root.logger=INFO,console
```

DistCp

License	Apache License, Version 2.0
Activity	Low
Purpose	Data movement between Hadoop clusters
Official Page	*http://hadoop.apache.org/docs/r1.2.1/distcp2.html*
Hadoop Integration	Fully Integrated

If you have a Hadoop cluster and worry what would happen if the entire cluster became unusable, you have a disaster recovery (DR) or continuity of operations (COOP) issue. There are several strategies for dealing with this. One solution might be to load all data into both a primary Hadoop cluster and a backup cluster located remotely from the primary cluster. This is frequently called dual ingest. Then you would have to run every job on the primary cluster on the remote cluster to keep the result files in sync. While feasible, this is managerially complex. You might want to consider using a built-in part of Apache Hadoop called DistCp. Short for distributed copy, DistCP is the primary tool for moving data between Hadoop clusters. You may want to use DistCp for other reasons as well, such as moving data from a test or development cluster to a production cluster. Commercial Hadoop distributions have tools to deal with DR and COOP. Some are built on top of DistCp.

Tutorial Links

Likely as a result of the single-minded simplicity of DistCp, there aren't a whole lot of dedicated tutorials about the technology. Readers who are interested in digging deeper are invited to start with the official project page (*http://bit.ly/1AmEdG0*).

Example Code

Here's how you would copy a file named *source-file* in the source system n1 in the *source-dir* to destination system n2, where the hostnames n1 and n2 are the hostnames of the node on which the Name-Node lives for the source and destination, respectively. If you were using this code snippet in a DR situation, the *source-dir* and *dest-dir* would be the same, as would be the *source-file* and *dest-file*:

```
$ hadoop distcp hdfs://n1:8020/source-dir/source-file \
                hdfs://n2:8020/dest-dir/dest-file
```

Storm

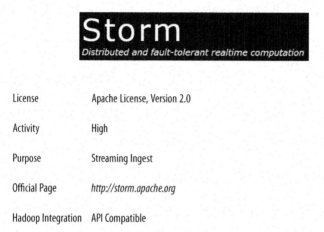

Storm
Distributed and fault-tolerant realtime computation

License	Apache License, Version 2.0
Activity	High
Purpose	Streaming Ingest
Official Page	*http://storm.apache.org*
Hadoop Integration	API Compatible

Many of the technologies in the big data ecosystem, including Hadoop MapReduce, are built with very large tasks in mind. These systems are designed to perform work in batches, bundling groups of smaller tasks into larger tasks and distributing those large tasks.

While batch processing is an effective strategy for performing complex analysis of very large amounts of data in a distributed and fault-tolerant fashion, it's ill-suited for processing data in real time. This is where a system like Storm comes in. Storm follows a stream processing model rather than a batch processing model. This means it's designed to quickly perform relatively simple transformations of very large numbers of small records.

In Storm, a workflow is called a "topology," with inputs called "spouts" and transformations called "bolts." It's important to note that Storm topologies are very different from MapReduce jobs, because jobs have a beginning and an end while topologies do not. The intent is that once you define a topology, data will continue to stream in from your spout and be processed through a series of bolts.

Tutorial Links

In addition to the official Storm tutorial (*http://bit.ly/1FyPYt9*), there is an excellent set of starter resources in GitHub in the Storm-Starter (*http://bit.ly/1Ac5fl5*) project.

Example Code

In this example, we're going to build a topology that reads comma-delimited reviews from a ReviewSpout and keeps track of the number of times each title is reviewed. Defining a Storm topology can get a little involved, so we'll just cover the highlights.

The first step of defining a topology is to define our inputs. We do this by associating a spout with our topology. This spout will be responsible for reading data from some source, such as a Twitter or an RSS feed.

Once we have our spout defined, we can start defining bolts. Bolts are responsible for processing our data. In this case, we have two bolts—the first extracts the movie title from a review, and the second counts the number of times an individual title appears:

```
TopologyBuilder builder = new TopologyBuilder();
builder.setSpout("review_spout", new ReviewSpout(), 10);
builder.setBolt("extract_title", new TitleBolt(), 8);
builder.setBolt("count", new TitleCount(), 15);

//Build the "conf" object and configure it appropriately
// for your job
...

StormSubmitter.submitTopology("review_counter", conf,
builder.createTopology());
```

Spouts and bolts can be authored in a variety of languages, and you can even mix languages in an individual topology. For example, we authored our topology in Java, but we're going to write one of our bolts in Python. This bolt extracts the film title from a review by splitting the review on commas and retrieving the second field:

```
import storm

class TitleBolt(storm.BasicBolt):
    def process(self, tuple):
        words = tuple.values[0].split(",")
        storm.emit([words[1]])

TitleBolt().run()
```

## CHAPTER 7

Security, Access Control, and Auditing

When Hadoop was getting started, its basic security model might have been described as "build a fence around an elephant, but once inside the fence, security is a bit lax." While the HDFS has access control mechanisms, security is a bit of an afterthought in the Hadoop world. Recently, as Hadoop has become much more mainstream, security issues are being addressed through the development of new tools, such as Sentry and Knox, as well as established mechanisms like Kerberos.

Large, well-established computing systems have methods for access and authorization, encryption, and audit logging, as required by HIPAA, FISMA, and PCI requirements.

Authentication answers the question, "Who are you?" Traditional strong authentication methods include Kerberos, Lightweight Directory Access Protocol (LDAP), and Active Directory (AD). These are done outside of Hadoop, usually at the client site, or within the web server if appropriate.

Authorization answers the question, "What can you do?" Here Hadoop is spread all over the place. For example, the MapReduce job queue system stores its authorization in a different way than HDFS, which uses a common read/write/execute permission for users/groups/other. HBase has column family and table-level authorization, and Accumulo has cell-level authorization.

Data protection generally refers to encryption, both at rest or in transit. HTTP, RPC, JDBC, and ODBC all provide encryption in transit or over the wire. HDFS currently has no native encryption, but there is a proposal in process to include this in a future release.

Governance and auditing are now done component-wise in Hadoop. There are some basic mechanisms in HDFS and MapReduce, whereas Hive metastore provides logging services and Oozie provides logging for its job-management service.

This guide (*http://bit.ly/1zLTzU9*) is a good place to start reading about a more secure Hadoop.

Recently, as Hadoop has become much more mainstream, these issues are being addressed through the development of new tools, such as Sentry (described on page 103), Kerberos (described on page 105), and Knox (described on page 107).

Sentry

License	Apache License, Version 2.0
Activity	High
Purpose	Provide a base level of authorization in Hadoop
Official Page	*https://incubator.apache.org/projects/sentry.html*
Hadoop Integration	API Compatible Incubator project (work in progress)

If you need authentication services in Hadoop, one possibility is Sentry, an Apache Incubator project to provide authentication services to components in the Hadoop ecosystem. The system currently defines a set of policy rules in a file that defines groups, mapping of groups to rules, and rules that define the privileges of groups to resources. You can think of this as role-based access control (RBAC). Your application then calls a Sentry API with the name of the user, the resource the user wishes to access, and the manner of access. The Sentry policy engine then sees if the user belongs to a group that has a role that enables it to use the resource in the manner requested. It returns a binary yes/no answer to the application, which can then take the appropriate response.

At the moment, this is filesystem-based and works with Hive and Impala out of the box. Other components can utilitze the API. One shortcoming of this system is that one could write a rogue MapReduce program that can access the data that would be restricted by using the Hive interface to the data.

Incubator projects are not part of the official Hadoop distribution and should not be used in production systems.

Tutorial Links

There are a pair of excellent posts on the official Apache blog. The first post (*http://bit.ly/1EYsznm*) provides an overview of the technology, while the second post (*http://bit.ly/1KJe9rE*) is a getting-started guide.

Example Code

Configuration of Sentry is fairly complex and beyond the scope of this book. The Apache blog posts referenced here an excellent resource for readers looking to get started with the technology.

There is very succinct example code in this Apache blog tutorial (*http://bit.ly/1KJe9rE*).

Kerberos

License	MIT license
Activity	High
Purpose	Secure Authentication
Official Page	*http://web.mit.edu/kerberos*
Hadoop Integration	API Compatible

One common way to authenticate in a Hadoop cluster is with a security tool called Kerberos. Kerberos is a network-based tool distributed by the Massachusetts Institute of Technology to provide strong authentication based upon supplying secure encrypted tickets between clients requesting access to servers providing the access.

The model is fairly simple. Clients register with the Kerberos key distribution center (KDC) and share their password. When a client wants access to a resource like a file server, it sends a request to the KDC with some portion encryped with this password. The KDC attempts to decrypt this material. If successful, it sends back a ticket generating ticket (TGT) to the client, which has material encrypted with its special passcode. When the client receives the TGT, it sends a request back to the KDC with a request for access to the file server. The KDC sends back a ticket with bits encrypted with the file server's passcode. From then on, the client and the file server use this ticket to authenticate.

The notion is that the file server, which might be very busy with many client requests, is not bogged down with the mechanics of keeping many user passcodes. It just shares its passcode with the

KDC and uses the ticket the client has received from the KDC to authenticate.

Kerberos is thought to be tedious to set up and maintain. To this end, there is some active work in the Hadoop community to present a simpler and more effective authentication mechanism.

Tutorial Links

This lecture (*http://youtu.be/kp5d8Yv3-0c*) provides a fairly concise and easy-to-follow description of the technology.

Example Code

An effective Kerberos installation can be a daunting task and is well beyond the scope of this book. Many operating system vendors provide a guide for configuring Kerberos. For more information, refer to the guide for your particular OS.

Knox

KNOX

License	Apache License, Version 2.0
Activity	Medium
Purpose	Secure Gateway
Official Page	*https://knox.apache.org*
Hadoop Integration	Fully Integrated

Securing a Hadoop cluster is often a complicated, time-consuming endeavor fraught with trade-offs and compromise. The largest contributing factor to this challenge is that Hadoop is made of a variety of different technologies, each of which has its own idea of security.

One common approach to securing a cluster is to simply wrap the environment with a firewall ("fence the elephant"). This may have been acceptable in the early days when Hadoop was largely a stand-alone tool for data scientists and information analysts, but the Hadoop of today is part of a much larger big data ecosystem and interfaces with many tools in a variety of ways. Unfortunately, each tool seems to have its own public interface, and if a security model happens to be present, it's often different from that of any other tool. The end result of all this is that users who want to maintain a secure environment find themselves fighting a losing battle of poking holes in firewalls and attempting to manage a large variety of separate user lists and tool configurations.

Knox is designed to help combat this complexity. It is a single gateway that lives between systems external to your Hadoop cluster and those internal to your cluster. It also provides a single security interface with authorization, authentication, and auditing (AAA) capabilies that interface with many standard systems, such as Active Directory and LDAP.

Tutorial Links

The folks at Hortonworks have put together a very concise guide (*http://bit.ly/1uEYW76*) for getting a minimal Knox gateway going. If you're interested in digging a little deeper, the official quick-start guide, which can be found on the Knox home page (*https://knox.apache.org*), provides a considerable amount of detail.

Example Code

Even a simple configuration of Knox is beyond the scope of this book. Interested readers are encouraged to check out the tutorials and quickstarts.

## CHAPTER 8

Cloud Computing and Virtualization

Most Hadoop clusters today run on "real iron"—that is, on small, Intel-based computers running some variant of the Linux operating system with directly attached storage. However, you might want to try this in a cloud or virtual environment. While virtualization usually comes with some degree of performance degradation, you may find it minimal for your task set or that it's a worthwhile trade-off for the benefits of cloud computing; these benefits include low up-front costs and the ability to scale up (and down sometimes) as your dataset and analytic needs change.

By cloud computing, we'll follow guidelines established by the National Institute of Standards and Technology (NIST), whose definition of cloud computing you'll find here (*http://bit.ly/nist-cloud-compute*). A Hadoop cluster in the cloud will have:

- On-demand self-service
- Network access
- Resource sharing
- Rapid elasticity
- Measured resource service

While these resource need not exist virtually, in practice, they usually do.

Virtualization means creating virtual, as opposed to real, computing entities. Frequently, the virtualized object is an operating system on which software or applications are overlaid, but storage and networks can also be virtualized. Lest you think that virtualization is a relatively new computing technology, in 1972 IBM released VM/370, in which the 370 mainframe could be divided into many small, single-user virtual machines. Currently, Amazon Web Services is likely the most well-known cloud-computing facility. For a brief explanation of virtualization, look here on Wikipedia (*http://bit.ly/1Chsx4b*).

The official Hadoop perspective on cloud computing and virtualization is explained on this Wikipedia page (*http://bit.ly/1yhiNoe*). One guiding principle of Hadoop is that data analytics should be run on nodes in the cluster close to the data. Why? Transporting blocks of data in a cluster diminishes performance. Because blocks of HDFS files are normally stored three times, it's likely that MapReduce can chose nodes to run your jobs on datanodes on which the data is stored. In a naive virtual environment, the physical location of the data is not known, and in fact, the real physical storage may be someplace that is not on any node in the cluster at all.

While it's admittedly from a VMware perspective, good background reading on virtualizing Hadoop can be found here (*http://vmw.re/1KJesCR*).

In this chapter, you'll read about some of the open source software that facilitates cloud computing and virtualization. There are also proprietary solutions, but they're not covered in this edition of the *Field Guide to Hadoop*.

Serengeti

License	Apache License, Version 2.0
Activity	Medium
Purpose	Hadoop Virtualization
Official Page	*http://www.projectserengeti.org*
Hadoop Integration	No Integration

If your organization uses VMware's vSphere as the basis of the virtualization strategy, then Serengeti provides you with a method of quickly building Hadoop clusters in your environment. Admittedly, vSphere is a proprietary environment, but the code to run Hadoop in this environment is open source. Though Serengeti is not affiliated with the Apache Software Foundation (which operates many of the other Hadoop-related projects), many people have successfully used it in deployments.

Why virtualize Hadoop at all? Historically, Hadoop clusters have run on commodity servers (i.e., Intel x86 machines with their own set of disks running the Linux OS). When scheduling jobs, Hadoop made use of the location of data in the HDFS (described on page 3) to run the code as close to the data as possible, preferably in the same node, to minimize the amount of data transferred across the network. In many virtualized environments, the directly attached storage is replaced by a common storage device like a storage area network (SAN) or a network attached storage (NAS). In these environments, there is no notion of locality of storage.

There are good reasons for virtualizing Hadoop, and there seem to be many Hadoop clusters running on public clouds today:

- Speed of quickly spinning up a cluster. You don't need to order and configure hardware.

- Ability to quickly increase and reduce the size of the cluster to meet demand for services.

- Resistance and recovery from failures managed by the virtualization technology.

And there are some disadvantages:

- MapReduce and YARN assume complete control of machine resources. This is not true in a virtualized environment.

- Data layout is critical, so excessive disk head movement may occur and the normal triple mirroring is critical for data protection. A good virtualization strategy must do the same. Some do, some don't.

You'll need to weigh the advantages and disadvantages to decide if Virtual Hadoop is appropriate for your projects.

Tutorial Links

Background reading on virtualizing Hadoop can be found at:

- "Deploying Hadoop with Serengeti" (*http://bit.ly/1CVnHPs*)
- The Virtual Hadoop wiki (*http://bit.ly/1yhiNoe*)
- "Hadoop Virtualization Extensions on VMware vSphere 5" (*http://vmw.re/1tOgJbj*)
- "Virtualizing Apache Hadoop" (*http://vmw.re/1KJesCR*)

Docker

License	Apache License, Version 2.0
Activity	High
Purpose	Container to run apps, including Hadoop nodes
Official Page	*https://www.docker.com*
Hadoop Integration	No Integration

You may have heard the buzz about Docker and containerized applications. A little history may help here. Virtual machines were a large step forward in both cloud computing and infrastructure as a service (IaaS). Once a Linux virtual machine was created, it took less than a minute to spin up a new one, whereas building a Linux hardware machine could take hours. But there are some drawbacks. If you built a cluster of 100 VMs, and needed to change an OS parameter or update something in your Hadoop environment, you would need to do it on each of the 100 VMs.

To understand Docker's advantages, you'll find it useful to understand its lineage. First came chroot jails, in which Unix subsystems could be built that were restricted to a smaller namespace than the entire Unix OS. Then came Solaris containers in which users and programs could be restricted to zones, each protected from the others with many virtualized resources. Linux containers are roughly the same as Solaris containers, but for the Linux OS rather than Solaris. Docker arose as a technology to do lightweight virtualization for applications. The Docker container sits on top of Linux OS resources and just houses the application code and whatever it depends upon over and above OS resources. Thus Dockers enjoys the resource isolation and resource allocation features of a virtual machine, but is much more portable and lightweight. A full description of Docker is beyoond the scope of this book, but recently attempts have been made to run Hadoop nodes in a Docker environment.

Docker is new. It's not clear that this is ready for a large Hadoop production environment.

Tutorial Links

The Docker folks have made it easy to get started with an interactive tutorial (*http://bit.ly/1DFq08i*). Readers who want to know more about the container technology behind Docker will find this developerWorks article (*http://ibm.co/1E9F5MY*) particularly interesting.

Example Code

The tutorials do a very good job giving examples of running Docker. This Pivotal blog post (*http://bit.ly/1EYt4hr*) illustrates an example of deploying Hadoop on Docker.

Whirr

License	Apache License, Version 2.0
Activity	Low
Purpose	Cluster Deployment
Official Page	*https://whirr.apache.org*
Hadoop Integration	API Compatible

Building a big data cluster is an expensive, time-consuming, and complicated endeavor that often requires coordination between many teams. Sometimes you just need to spin up a cluster to test a capability or prototype a new idea. Cloud services like Amazon EC2 or Rackspace Cloud Servers provide a way to get that done. Unfortunately, different providers have very different interfaces for working with their services, so once you've developed some automation around the process of building and tearing down these test clusters, you've effectively locked yourself in with a single service provider. Apache Whirr provides a standard mechanism for working with a handful of different service providers. This allows you to easily change cloud providers or to share configurations with other teams that do not use the same cloud provider.

The most basic building block of Whirr is the instance template. *Instance templates* define a purpose; for example, there are templates for the Hadoop jobtracker, ZooKeeper, and HBase region nodes. *Recipes* are one step up the stack from templates and define a cluster. For example, a *recipe* for a simple data-processing cluster might call for deploying a Hadoop NameNode, a Hadoop jobtracker, a couple ZooKeeper servers, an HBase master, and a handful of HBase region servers.

Tutorial Links

The official Apache Whirr website (*https://whirr.apache.org/*) provides a couple of excellent tutorials. The Whirr in 5 minutes (*http://bit.ly/17gPvAF*) tutorial provides the exact commands necessary to spin up and shut down your first cluster. The quick-start guide (*http://bit.ly/Whirr_quick-start*) is a little more involved, walking through what happens during each stage of the process.

Example Code

In this case, we're going to deploy the simple data cluster we described earlier to an Amazon EC2 account we've already established.

The first step is to build our recipe file (we'll call this file *field_guide.properties*):

```
# field_guide.properties

# The name we'll give this cluster,
# this gets communicated with the cloud service provider
whirr.cluster-name=field_guide

# Because we're just testing
# we'll put all the masters on one single machine
# and build only three worker nodes
whirr.instance-templates= \
1 zookeeper+hadoop-namenode \
+hadoop-jobtracker \
+hbase-master,\
3 hadoop-datanode \
+hadoop-tasktracker \
+hbase-regionserver

# We're going to deploy the cluster to Amazon EC2
whirr.provider=aws-ec2

# The identity and credential mean different things
# depending on the provider you choose.
# Because we're using EC2, we need to enter our
# Amazon access key ID and secret access key;
# these are easily available from your provider.
whirr.identity=<your identity here>
whirr.credential=<your key here>

# The credentials we'll use to access the cluster.
# In this case, Whirr will create a user named field_guide_user
# on each of the machines it spins up and
```

```
# we'll use our ssh public key to connect as that user.
whirr.cluster-user=field_guide_user
whirr.private-key-file=${sys:user.home}/.ssh/id_rsa
whirr.public-key-file=${sys:user.home}/.ssh/id_rsa

We're now ready to deploy our cluster.
# In order to do so we simply run whirr with the
# "launch cluster" argument and pass it our recipe:
$ whirr launch-cluster --config field_guide.properties

Once we're done with the cluster and we want to tear it down
# we run a similar command,
# this time passing the aptly named "destroy-cluster" argument:
$ whirr destroy-cluster --config field_guide.properties
```

About the Authors

Kevin Sitto is a field solutions engineer with Pivotal Software, providing consulting services to help folks understand and address their big data needs.

He lives in Maryland with his wife and two kids, and enjoys making homebrew beer when he's not writing books about big data.

Marshall Presser is a field chief technology officer for Pivotal Software and is based in McLean, Virginia. In addition to helping customers solve complex analytic problems with the Greenplum Database, he leads the Hadoop Virtual Field Team, working on issues of integrating Hadoop with relational databases.

Prior to coming to Pivotal (formerly Greenplum), he spent 12 years at Oracle, specializing in high availability, business continuity, clustering, parallel database technology, disaster recovery, and large-scale database systems. Marshall has also worked for a number of hardware vendors implementing clusters and other parallel architectures. His background includes parallel computation and operating system/compiler development, as well as private consulting for organizations in healthcare, financial services, and federal and state governments.

Marshall holds a B.A. in mathematics and an M.A. in economics and statistics from the University of Pennsylvania, and a M.Sc. in computing from Imperial College, London.

Colophon

The animals on the cover of *Field Guide to Hadoop* are the O'Reilly animals most associated with the technologies covered in this book: the skua seabird, lowland paca, hydra porpita pacifica, trigger fish, African elephant, Pere David's deer, European wildcat, ruffed grouse, and chimpanzee.

Many of the animals on O'Reilly covers are endangered; all of them are important to the world. To learn more about how you can help, go to *animals.oreilly.com*.

The cover fonts are URW Typewriter and Guardian Sans. The text font is Adobe Minion Pro; the heading font is Adobe Myriad Condensed; and the code font is Dalton Maag's Ubuntu Mono.

Get even more for your money.

Join the O'Reilly Community, and register the O'Reilly books you own. It's free, and you'll get:

- $4.99 ebook upgrade offer
- 40% upgrade offer on O'Reilly print books
- Membership discounts on books and events
- Free lifetime updates to ebooks and videos
- Multiple ebook formats, DRM FREE
- Participation in the O'Reilly community
- Newsletters
- Account management
- 100% Satisfaction Guarantee

Signing up is easy:

1. Go to: oreilly.com/go/register
2. Create an O'Reilly login.
3. Provide your address.
4. Register your books.

Note: English-language books only

To order books online:
oreilly.com/store

For questions about products or an order:
orders@oreilly.com

To sign up to get topic-specific email announcements and/or news about upcoming books, conferences, special offers, and new technologies:
elists@oreilly.com

For technical questions about book content:
booktech@oreilly.com

To submit new book proposals to our editors:
proposals@oreilly.com

O'Reilly books are available in multiple DRM-free ebook formats. For more information:
oreilly.com/ebooks

CPSIA information can be obtained at www.ICGtesting.com
Printed in the USA
BVOW08s1632080315

390742BV00004B/6/P

9 781491 947937